INSTINCT
An Enduring Problem in Psychology

SELECTED READINGS

Edited by
ROBERT C. BIRNEY
Amherst College
AND
RICHARD C. TEEVAN
Bucknell University

AN INSIGHT BOOK

D. VAN NOSTRAND COMPANY, INC.
PRINCETON, NEW JERSEY
TORONTO   LONDON
NEW YORK

PROVIDENCE
COLLEGE
LIBRARY

D. VAN NOSTRAND COMPANY, INC.
120 Alexander St., Princeton, New Jersey
(Principal Office)
24 West 40 Street, New York 18, New York

D. VAN NOSTRAND COMPANY, LTD.
358, Kensington High Street, London, W.14, England

D. VAN NOSTRAND COMPANY (Canada), LTD.
25 Hollinger Road, Toronto 16, Canada

COPYRIGHT © 1961, BY
D. VAN NOSTRAND COMPANY, INC.

Published simultaneously in Canada by
D. VAN NOSTRAND COMPANY (Canada), LTD.

No reproduction in any form of this book, in whole or in part (except for brief quotation in critical articles or reviews) may be made without written authorization from the publishers

PRINTED IN THE UNITED STATES OF AMERICA

Foreword

In the field of psychology we believe that the student ought to get the "feel" of experimentation by reading original source materials. In this way he can acquire a better understanding of the discipline by seeing scientific ideas grow and change. However, one of the main problems in teaching is the limited availability of these sources, which communicate most effectively the personality of the author and the excitement of ongoing research.

For these reasons we have decided to edit several books,* each devoted to a particular problem in psychology. In every case we attempt to select problems that have been and are controversial—that have been and still are alive. We intend to present these problems as a set of selected original articles which are arranged in historical order and in order of progress in the field. We believe that it is important for the student to see that theories and researches build on what has gone before; that one study leads to another, that theory leads to research and then to revision of theory. We believe that *telling* the student this does not make the same kind of impression as letting him see it happen in actuality. This is the rationale behind this series of problems books. Editor's remarks are kept to the absolute minimum. The idea is for the student to read and build ideas for himself. (It should also be pointed out that articles deemed too technical are not included.)

Suggestions for Use

These readings books can be used by the student in either of two ways. They are organized so that, with the help of the instructor (or of the students if used in seminars), a topic can be covered at length and in depth. This would necessitate lectures or discussions on articles not covered in the series to fill in the gaps. On the other hand, each book taken alone will give a student a good idea of the problem being covered and its historical back-

* (Pub. note: to be a sub-series within the Insight Book Series)

ground as well as its present state and the direction it seems to be taking. At the risk of being repetitious, we would like to say again that we believe it is important for the student to see how theories and researches lead to other researches and revision of theories. It is also important for the student to become familiar with significant researches at first hand. It is to these ideas that this sub-series on enduring problems in psychology is dedicated.

Amherst, Mass. R.C.B.
Lewisburg, Pa. R.C.T.
January, 1961

Contents

1. INSTINCT — 1
   by William James
2. THE MISUSE OF THE CONCEPT OF INSTINCT — 13
   by Luther L. Bernard
3. THE GENESIS OF THE CAT'S RESPONSE TO THE RAT — 20
   by Zing Yang Kuo
4. FURTHER STUDY ON THE BEHAVIOR OF THE CAT TOWARDS THE RAT — 27
   by Zing Yang Kuo
5. THE DEVELOPMENT OF BEHAVIOR IN VERTEBRATES EXPERIMENTALLY REMOVED FROM THE INFLUENCE OF EXTERNAL STIMULATION — 35
   by Leonard Carmichael
6. IMPRINTING — 52
   by Konrad Z. Lorenz
7. EXPERIMENTAL ANALYSIS OF BEHAVIOR — 65
   by Karl S. Lashley
8. INTRODUCTION OF MATING BEHAVIOR IN MALE AND FEMALE CHICKS FOLLOWING INJECTION OF SEX HORMONES — 77
   by Gladwyn K. Noble and Arthur Zitrin
9. THE EFFECTS OF MEPROBAMATE ON IMPRINTING IN WATERFOWL — 90
   by Eckhard H. Hess
10. AN ATTEMPT AT SYNTHESIS — 104
    by Nikolaas Tinbergen
11. THE INHERITANCE OF BEHAVIOUR: BEHAVIOURAL DIFFERENCES IN FIFTEEN MOUSE STRAINS — 121
    by William R. Thompson
12. GENETIC DIFFERENCES IN DOGS. A CASE OF MAGNIFICATION BY THRESHOLDS AND BY HABIT FORMATION — 135
    by John P. Scott and Margaret S. Charles

| 13. | PROBLEMS RAISED BY INSTINCT THEORIES
by Daniel S. Lehrman | 152 |
| 14. | THE DESCENT OF INSTINCT
by Frank A. Beach | 165 |

Introduction

This volume of selected experiments and articles provides the reader with a firsthand experience with the literature produced by psychologists and workers in the biological sciences who have addressed themselves to the problems posed by the order and regularity of the behavior of infrahumans. Though a problem faced by philosophers since antiquity, as Beach succinctly shows, the advent of a scientific psychology insured that the many complex and mysterious behavior patterns which reliably appear in the life cycle of a species would become a primary field of study. We begin with William James because his treatment of the subject gives the first hint that empirical studies were to become increasingly important as a means of resolving issues, while his theoretical treatment sets the question as one of learning *vs.* heredity—the form it was to have for half a century.

Posing the question this way determined the design of experiments. One of the two variables had to be controlled while variation in the other was observed. It is interesting that those experiments which were to become classic examples of this technique led their authors to the position that such a statement of the problem was much too simple to do justice to the processes being studied. Both Kuo and Carmichael make a strong plea for the recasting of the problem as one of identification and study of both physiological and situational variables and their interaction. A similar conclusion is reached by Lashley in 1938.

But there were difficulties in the way of this step. Bernard's review showed that theorists who preferred the instinct-learning distinction were those who felt the phenomena of instinctual events to be self-evident. Everyone knew that birds build nests without practice, and no amount of reductionism could possibly account for such a complex end product as an oriole's nest. Indeed, it was the logical assault on the term which damped down its use during the thirties, rather than the wise counsel of those most involved in research.

A second difficulty also appeared about this time with the appearance of increasingly ingenious and startling findings of the ethologists. Lorenz, and later Tinbergen, had been involved in a reductive study of complex behavior that commanded the respect of the most empirically minded psychologists. But they both felt that the discovery of critical developmental periods had uncovered basic processes which did have much of the character demanded by a rigorous definition of the term instinct. Hence we find in Tinbergen a reintroduction of the term.

By this time other approaches to the problems were being tried. Hormone injections, drug effects, and comparison of genetically distinct breeds of dogs, or strains of mice, are here offered as representative of the growing literature which takes as its independent variable one of the many possible physical determinants. It seems fair to say that most of these researchers feel their work is crude in the sense that the properties of the independent variables themselves are not well understood, let alone their effects on behavior. But there can be no doubt that the push to delineate the many proccesses involved in the unfolding of organic behavior has begun.

Lehrman's summary article and attack on the theorizing of Tinbergen and Lorenz provides us with a detailed statement of the case for process analysis. He concedes nothing to those who argue for the irreductive character of certain developmental events. His discussion of the pecking response in the chick gives an excellent example of the direction which research is now taking. Finally, we end with Beach's ideas on the course of events which have preceded the limited span of years covered by these selections. His own affirmation that the problem was misstated, and that it has suffered at the hands of amateurs within psychology, provides a lesson in the history of a science which is hardly old enough to have a history.

The readings in this volume were selected to indicate representative thinking on the concept of instinct. Even so, the selections of the latter half of the book are quite arbitrary. For the first time this issue is now under vigorous empirical attack and we may expect a rising volume of publications. It seems likely that with this increase in knowledge the issue of the proper concept for certain classes of variables will fade away. The variables themselves will take the center stage in future works of this kind.

Instinct

WILLIAM JAMES

From *Principles of Psychology* by William James; Henry Holt and Company, New York, 1890, pp. 383-393 (excerpted).

This chapter has already appeared (almost exactly as it is now printed) in the form of magazine articles in Scribner's Magazine and in the Popular Science Monthly for 1887.

INSTINCT *is usually defined as the faculty of acting in such a way as to produce certain ends, without foresight of the ends, and without previous education in the performance.* That instincts, as thus defined, exist on an enormous scale in the animal kingdom needs no proof. They are the functional correlatives of structure. With the presence of a certain organ goes, one may say, almost always a native aptitude for its use.

"Has the bird a gland for the secretion of oil? She knows instinctively how to press the oil from the gland, and apply it to the feather. Has the rattlesnake the grooved tooth and gland of poison? He knows without instruction how to make both structure and function most effective against his enemies. Has the silkworm the function of secreting the fluid silk? At the proper time she winds the cocoon such as she has never seen, as thousands before have done, and thus without instruction, pattern or experience, forms a safe abode for herself in the period of transformation. Has the hawk talons? She knows by instinct how to wield them effectively against the helpless quarry." *

A very common way of talking about these admirably definite tendencies to act is by naming abstractly the

* P. A. Chadbourne: *Instinct*, p. 28 (New York, 1872).

purpose they subserve, such as self-preservation, or defence, or care for eggs and young—and saying the animal has an instinctive fear of death or love of life, or that she has an instinct of self-preservation, or an instinct of maternity and the like. But this represents the animal as obeying abstractions which not once in a million cases is it possible it can have framed. The strict physiological way of interpreting the facts leads to far clearer results. *The actions we call instinctive all conform to the general reflex type*; they are called forth by determinate sensory stimuli in contact with the animal's body, or at a distance in his environment. The cat runs after the mouse, runs or shows fight before the dog, avoids falling from walls and trees, shuns fire and water, etc., not because he has any notion either of life or of death, or of self, or of preservation. He has probably attained to no one of these conceptions in such a way as to react definitely upon it. He acts in each case separately, and simply because he cannot help it; being so framed that when that particular running thing called a mouse appears in his field of vision he *must* pursue; that when that particular barking and obstreperous thing called a dog appears there he *must* retire, if at a distance, and scratch if close by; that he *must* withdraw his feet from water and his face from flame, etc. His nervous system is to a great extent a preorganized bundle of such reactions—they are as fatal as sneezing, and as exactly correlated to their special excitants as it is to its own. Although the naturalist may, for his own convenience, class these reactions under general heads, he must not forget that in the animal it is a particular sensation or perception or image which calls them forth.

At first this view astounds us by the enormous number of special adjustments it supposes animals to possess ready-made in anticipation of the outer things among which they are to dwell. *Can* mutual dependence be so intricate and go so far? Is each thing born fitted to particular other things, and to them exclusively, as locks are fitted to their keys? Undoubtedly this must be believed to be so. Each nook and cranny of creation, down to our very skin and entrails, has its living inhabitants, with organs suited to the place, to devour and digest the food it harbors and to meet the dangers it conceals; and the minuteness of adaptations thus shown in the way of *structure* knows no bounds. Even so are there no bounds to the minuteness of adaptation in the way of *conduct* which the several inhabitants display.

The older writings on instinct are ineffectual wastes of words, because their authors never came down to this definite and simple point of view, but smothered everything in vague wonder at the clairvoyant and prophetic power of the animals—so superior to anything in man—and at the beneficence of God in endowing them with such a gift. But God's beneficence endows them, first of all, with a nervous system; and, turning our attention to this, makes instinct immediately appear neither more nor less wonderful than all the other facts of life.

Every instinct is an impulse. Whether we shall call such impulses as blushing, sneezing, coughing, smiling, or dodging, or keeping time to music, instincts or not, is a mere matter of terminology. The process is the same throughout. In his delightfully fresh and interesting work, *Der Thierische Wille*, Herr G. H. Schneider subdivides impulses (*Triebe*) into sensation-impulses, perception-impulses, and idea-impulses. To crouch from cold is a sensation-impulse; to turn and follow, if we see people running one way, is a perception-impulse; to cast about for cover, if it begins to blow and rain, is an imagination-impulse. A single complex instinctive action may involve successively the awakening of impulses of all three classes. Thus a hungry lion starts to *seek* prey by the awakening in him of imagination coupled with desire; he begins to *stalk* it when, on eye, ear, or nostril, he gets an impression of its presence at a certain distance; he *springs* upon it, either when the booty takes alarm and flees, or when the distance is sufficiently reduced; he proceeds to *tear* and *devour* it the moment he gets a sensation of its contact with his claws and fangs. Seeking, stalking, springing, and devouring are just so many different kinds of muscular contraction, and neither kind is called forth by the stimulus appropriate to the other.

Schneider says of the hamster, which stores corn in

its hole: "If we analyze the propensity of storing, we find that it consists of three impulses: First, an impulse to *pick up* the nutritious object, due to perception; second, an impulse to *carry it off* into the dwelling-place, due to the idea of this latter; and, third, an impulse to *lay it down* there, due to the sight of the place. It lies in the nature of the hamster that it should never see a full ear of corn without feeling a desire to strip it; it lies in its nature to feel, as soon as its cheek-pouches are filled, an irresistible desire to hurry to its home; and finally, it lies in its nature that the sight of the storehouse should awaken the impulse to empty the cheeks" (p. 208).

In certain animals of a low order the feeling of having executed one impulsive step is such an indispensable part of the stimulus of the next one, that the animal cannot make any variation in the order of its performance.

Now, why do the various animals do what seem to us such strange things, in the presence of such outlandish stimuli? Why does the hen, for example, submit herself to the tedium of incubating such a fearfully uninteresting set of objects as a nestful of eggs, unless she have some sort of a prophetic inkling of the result? The only answer is *ad hominem*. We can only interpret the instincts of brutes by what we know of instincts in ourselves. Why do men always lie down, when they can, on soft beds rather than on hard floors? Why do they sit around the stove on a cold day? Why, in a room, do they place themselves, ninety-nine times out of a hundred, with their faces towards its middle rather than the wall? Why do they prefer saddle of mutton and champagne to hard-tack and ditch-water? Why does the maiden interest the youth so that everything about her seems more important and significant than anything else in the world? Nothing more can be said than that these are human ways, and that every creature *likes* its own ways, and takes to the following of them as a matter of course. Science may come and consider these ways, and find that most of them are useful. But it is not for the sake of their utility that they are followed, but because at the moment of following them we feel that that is the only appropriate thing to do. Not one man in a billion, when taking his dinner, ever thinks of utility. He eats because the food tastes good and makes him want more. If you ask him *why* he should want to eat more of what tastes like that, instead of revering you as a philosopher he will probably laugh at you for a fool. The connection between the savory sensation and the act it awakens is for him absolute and *selbstverständlich*, and '*a priori* synthesis' of the most perfect sort, needing no proof but its own evidence. It takes, in short, what Berkeley calls a mind debauched by learning to carry the process of making the natural seem strange, so far as to ask for the *why* of any instinctive human act. To the metaphysician alone can such questions occur as: Why do we smile, when pleased, and not scowl? Why are we unable to talk to a crowd as we talk to a single friend? Why does a particular maiden turn our wits so upside-down? The common man can only say, "*Of course* we smile, *of course* our heart palpitates at the sight of the crowd, *of course* we love the maiden, that beautiful soul clad in that perfect form, so palpably and flagrantly made from all eternity to be loved!*"*

And so, probably, does each animal feel about the particular things it tends to do in presence of particular objects. They, too, are *a priori* syntheses. To the lion it is the lioness which is made to be loved; to the bear, the she-bear. To the broody hen the notion would probably seem monstrous that there should be a creature in the world to whom a nestful of eggs was not the utterly fascinating and precious and never-to-be-too-much-sat-upon object which it is to her.*

---

* "It would be very simple-minded to suppose that bees follow their queen, and protect her and care for her, because they are aware that without her the hive would become extinct. The odor or the aspect of their queen is manifestly agreeable to the bees—that is why they love her so. Does not all true love base itself on agreeable perceptions much more than on representations of utility?" (G. H. Schneider, *Der Thierische Wille*, P. 187). A *priori*, there is no reason to suppose that *any* sensation might not in *some* animal cause *any* emotion and *any* impulse. To us it seems unnatural that an

Thus we may be sure that, however mysterious some animals' instincts may appear to us, our instincts will appear no less mysterious to them. And we may conclude that, to the animal which obeys it, every impulse and every step of every instinct shines with its own sufficient light, and seems at the moment the only eternally right and proper thing to do. It is done for its own sake exclusively. What voluptuous thrill may not shake a fly, when she at last discovers the one particular leaf, or carrion, or bit of dung, that out of all the world can stimulate her ovipositor to its discharge? Does not the discharge then seem to her the only fitting thing? And need she care or know anything about the future maggot and its food?

Since the *egg-laying instincts* are simple examples to consider, a few quotations about them from Schneider may be serviceable:

"The phenomenon so often talked about, so variously interpreted, so surrounded with mystification, that an insect should always lay her eggs in a spot appropriate to the nourishment of her young, is no more marvellous than the phenomenon that every animal pairs with a mate capable of bearing posterity, or feeds on materials capable of affording him nourishment. . . . Not only the choice of a place for laying the eggs, but all the various acts for depositing and protecting them, are occasioned by the perception of the proper object, and the relation of this perception to the various stages of maternal impulse. When the burying beetle perceives a carrion, she is not only impelled to approach it and lodge her eggs in it, but also to go through the movements requisite for burying it; just as a bird who sees his hen-bird is impelled to caress her, to strut around her, dance before her, or in some other way to woo her; just as a tiger, when he sees an antelope, is impelled to stalk it, to pounce upon it, and to strangle it. When the tailor-

---

odor should directly excite anger or fear; or a color, lust. Yet there are creatures to which some smells are quite as frightful as any sounds, and very likely others to which color is as much a sexual irritant as form.

bee cuts out pieces of rose-leaf, bends them, carries them into a caterpillar- or mouse-hole in trees or in the earth, covers their seams again with other pieces, and so makes a thimble-shaped case—when she fills this with honey and lays an egg in it, all these various appropriate expressions of her will are to be explained by supposing that at the time when the eggs are ripe within her, the appearance of a suitable caterpillar- or mouse-hole and the perception of rose-leaves are so correlated in the insect with the several impulses in question, that the performances follow as a matter of course when the perceptions take place. . . .

"The perception of the empty nest, or of a single egg, seems in birds to stand in such a close relation to the physiological functions of the oviparation that it serves as a direct stimulus to these functions, while the perception of a sufficient number of eggs has just the opposite effect. It is well known that hens and ducks lay more eggs if we keep removing them than if we leave them in the nest. The impulse to sit arises, as a rule, when a bird sees a certain number of eggs in her nest. If this number is not yet to be seen there, the ducks continue to lay, although they perhaps have laid twice as many eggs as they are accustomed to sit upon. . . . That sitting, also, is independent of any idea of purpose and is a pure perception-impulse is evident, among other things, from the fact that many birds, e.g. wild ducks, steal eggs from each other. . . . The bodily disposition to sit is, it is true, one condition (since broody hens will sit where there are no eggs), but the perception of the eggs is the other condition of the activity of the incubating impulse. The propensity of the cuckoo and of the cow-bird to lay their eggs in the nests of other species must also be interpreted as a pure perception-impulse. These birds have no bodily disposition to become broody, and there is therefore in them no connection between the perception of an egg and the impulse to sit upon it. Eggs ripen, however, in their oviducts, and the body tends to get rid of them. And since the two birds just named do not drop their eggs anywhere on the ground, but in nests, which are the only places where they may preserve the species, it might easily appear that such preservation of the species was what they had in view, and that they acted with full consciousness of the purpose. But this is not so. . . . The cuckoo is simply excited by the perception of quite determinate sorts of nest, which already contain eggs, to drop her own into them, and throw the others out, because this perception is a direct stimulus to these acts. It is impossible that she should have any notion of the other bird coming and sitting on her egg." *

INSTINCTS NOT ALWAYS BLIND OR INVARIABLE

Remember that nothing is said yet of the origin of instincts, but only of the constitution of those that exist fully formed. How stands it with the instincts of mankind?

Nothing is commoner than the remark that Man differs from lower creatures by the almost total absence of instincts, and the assumption of their work in him by 'reason.' A fruitless discussion might be waged on this point by two theorizers who were careful not to define their terms. 'Reason' might be used, as it often has been, since Kant, not as the mere power of 'inferring,' but also as a name for the *tendency to obey impulses* of a certain lofty sort, such as duty, or universal ends. And 'instinct' might have its significance so broadened as to cover all impulses whatever, even the impulse to act from the idea of a distant fact, as well as the impulse to act from a present sensation. Were the word instinct used in this broad way, it would of course be impossible to restrict it, as we began by doing, to actions done with no provision of an end. We must of course avoid a quarrel about words, and the facts of the case are really tolerably plain. Man has a far greater variety of *impulses* than any lower animal; and any one of these impulses, taken in itself, is as 'blind' as the lowest instinct can be; but, owing to man's memory, power of reflection, and power of inference, they come each one to be felt by him, after he has

* *Der Thierische Wille*, pp. 282-3.

once yielded to them and experienced their results, in connection with a *foresight* of those results. In this condition an impulse acted out may be said to be acted out, in part at least, *for the sake* of its results. It is obvious that *every instinctive act, in an animal with memory, must cease to be 'blind' after being once repeated*, and must be accompanied with foresight of its 'end' just so far as that end may have fallen under the animal's cognizance. An insect that lays her eggs in a place where she never sees them hatched must always do so 'blindly'; but a hen who has already hatched a brood can hardly be assumed to sit with perfect 'blindness' on her second nest. Some expectation of consequences must in every case like this be aroused; and this expectation, according as it is that of something desired or of something disliked, must necessarily either re-enforce or inhibit the mere impulse. The hen's idea of the chickens would probably encourage her to sit; a rat's memory, on the other hand, of a former escape from a trap would neutralize his impulse to take bait from anything that reminded him of that trap. If a boy sees a fat hopping-toad, he probably has incontinently an impulse (especially if with other boys) to smash the creature with a stone, which impulse we may suppose him blindly to obey. But something in the expression of the dying toad's clasped hands suggests the meanness of the act, or reminds him of sayings he has heard about the sufferings of animals being like his own; so that, when next he is tempted by a toad, an idea arises which, far from spurring him again to the torment, prompts kindly actions, and may even make him the toad's champion against less reflecting boys.

It is plain, then, that, *no matter how well endowed an animal may originally be in the way of instincts, his resultant actions will be much modified if the instincts combine with experience*, if in addition to impulses he have memories, associations, inferences, and expectations, on any considerable scale. An object O, on which he has an instinctive impulse to react in the manner A, would *directly* provoke him to that reaction. But O has meantime become for him a *sign* of the nearness of P, on which he has an equally strong impulse to react in the manner B, quite unlike A. So that when he meets O the immediate impulse A and the remote impulse B struggle in his breast for the mastery. The fatality and uniformity said to be characteristic of instinctive actions will be so little manifest that one might be tempted to deny to him altogether the possession of any instinct about the object O. Yet how false this judgment would be! The instinct about O is there; only by the complication of the associative machinery it has come into conflict with another instinct about P.

Here we immediately reap the good fruits of our simple physiological conception of what an instinct is. If it be a mere excito-motor impulse, due to the pre-existence of a certain 'reflex arc' in the nerve-centres of the creature, of course it must follow the law of all such reflex arcs. One liability of such arcs is to have their activity 'inhibited,' by other processes going on at the same time. It makes no difference whether the arc be organized at birth, or ripen spontaneously later, or be due to acquired habit, it must take its chances with all the other arcs, and sometimes succeed, and sometimes fail, in drafting off the currents through itself. The mystical view of an instinct would make it invariable. The physiological view would require it to show occasional irregularities in any animal in whom the number of separate instincts, and the possible entrance of the same stimulus into several of them, were great. And such irregularities are what every superior animal's instincts do show in abundance.*

* In the instincts of mammals, and even of lower creatures, the uniformity and infallibility which, a generation ago, were considered as essential characters do not exist. The minuter study of recent years has found continuity, transition, variation, and mistake, wherever it has looked for them, and decided that what is called an instinct is usually only a tendency to act in a way of which the *average* is pretty constant, but which need not be mathematically 'true.' Cf. on this point Darwin's *Origin of Species*: Romanes's *Mental Evol.*, Chaps. XI to XVI incl. and Appendix; W. L. Lindsay's *Mind in Lower Animals*, Vol. I, 133-141; II. Chaps. V, XX; and K. Semper's *Conditions of Existence in Animals*, where a great many instances will be found.

Wherever the mind is elevated enough to discriminate; wherever several distinct sensory elements must combine to discharge the reflex-arc; wherever, instead of plumping into action instantly at the first rough intimation of what *sort* of a thing is there, the agent waits to see which *one* of its kind it is and what the *circumstances* are of its appearance; wherever different individuals and different circumstances can impel him in different ways; wherever these are the conditions—we have a masking of the elementary constitution of the instinctive life. The whole story of our dealings with the lower wild animals is the history of our taking advantage of the way in which they judge of everything by its mere label, as it were, so as to ensnare or kill them. Nature, in them, has left matters in this rough way, and made them act *always* in the manner which would be *oftenest* right. There are more worms unattached to hooks than impaled upon them; therefore, on the whole, says Nature to her fishy children, bite at *every* worm and take your chances. But as her children get higher, and their lives more precious, she reduces the risks. Since what seems to be the same object may be now a genuine food and now a bait; since in gregarious species each individual may prove to be either the friend or the rival, according to the circumstances, of another; since any entirely unknown object may be fraught with weal or woe, *Nature implants contrary impulses to act on many classes of things,* and leaves it to slight alterations in the conditions of the individual case to decide which impulse shall carry the day. Thus, greediness and suspicion, curiosity and timidity, coyness and desire, bashfulness and vanity, sociability and pugnacity, seem to shoot over into each other as quickly, and to remain in as unstable equilibrium, in the higher birds and mammals as in man. They are all impulses, congenital, blind at first, and productive of motor reactions of a rigorously determinate sort. *Each one of them, then, is an instinct,* as instincts are commonly defined. *But they contradict each other*—'experience' in each particular opportunity of application usually deciding the issue. *The animal that exhibits them loses the 'instinctive' demeanor* and appears to lead a life of hesitation and choice, an intellectual life; *not, however, because he has no instincts—rather because he has so many that they block each other's path.*

Thus, then, without troubling ourselves about the words instinct and reason, we may confidently say that however uncertain man's reactions upon his environment may sometimes seem in comparison with those of lower creatures, the uncertainty is probably not due to their possession of any principles of action which he lacks. *On the contrary, man possesses all the impulses that they have, and a great many more besides.* In other words, there is no material antagonism between instinct and reason. Reason, per se, can inhibit no impulses; the only thing that can neutralize an impulse is an impulse the other way. Reason may, however, make an *inference which will excite the imagination so as to set loose* the impulse the other way; and thus, though the animal richest in reason might be also the animal richest in instinctive impulses too, he would never seem the fatal automaton which a *merely* instinctive animal would be.

2

The Misuse of the Concept of Instinct

LUTHER L. BERNARD

This selection is from *Introduction to Social Psychology*, Henry Holt and Company, Inc., New York, 1926, pp. 123-133 (excerpted).

Widespread use of the term instinct—Since the eighteenth century, when there was a strong attempt to understand the mechanisms by which human behavior actually occurred as well as to understand the environmental forces which produced behavior, there has been a good deal of emphasis upon the concept of instinct among the psychologists and ethicists. The concepts of conscience, sympathy, benevolence, and of other supposedly native impulses and behavior sets, were then already beginning to lose prestige. The nineteenth century saw these reputed causes of behavior pass out of legitimate social psychology as innate motives to conduct, although they remained as class terms for certain types of acquired dispositions. The demand was for more specific units of original behavior patterns, and the term instinct came largely to take the place of, and in some cases to include, the older projected entities which we have enumerated. At first the term instinct was itself used quite generally and loosely, as we have seen. Recognized specific instincts were few, but the general principle of instinct, or inborn behavior trait, was quite frequently invoked. Gradually the number of specific instincts increased, until late in the nineteenth and early in the twentieth centuries it became overwhelmingly large.

Examples of the misuse of the concept of instinct—

We have defined an instinct as a specific response to a specific stimulus, the neural pattern or structure mediating the response being inherited. If the pattern—that is, the neural connections—is not inherited, then the behavior pattern is acquired and not instinctive, however, definite and specific it may be. In the examples which follow these simple facts defining the nature of instinct will be seen to be violated.[1]

Classification of instincts—The absurdity of classifying the behavior patterns which have just been reviewed as instincts is sufficiently evident without further comment. But when one comes to make a classification of supposedly true instincts the problem of discrimination becomes more difficult. What are the instincts which actually do exist and operate in directing human behavior or enter into composite acquired behavior complexes? Various Utopians and social theorists with unilateral explanations of social conditions and problems often recognize only a single dominant instinct, with possibly a few subordinate or supporting instincts thrown in for good measure. Thus the so-called instincts of acquisitiveness, constructiveness, gregariousness, sex, fear, play, nutrition, etc., have at various times and under various circumstances served as the key to all human behavior. Freud, the psychoanalyst, recognizes only two fundamental instincts, sex and self-preservation, which he believes determine all human conduct. To these Jung and his followers add the herd instinct. McDougall, in his 'Social Psychology,' lists twelve such instincts, of which the first seven may be called primary and the others secondary. They are fear, repulsion, pugnacity, curiosity, self-abasement, self-assertion, parental, reproduction, gregariousness, emulation, acquisitiveness, hunger. To these he adds some general dispositions, which he does not call instincts, viz., sympathy, suggestion, play, and imitation. He does not even maintain that these general tendencies or dispositions are wholly or primarily inherited.

Many of the psychologists and others writing on in-

[1] Bernard then lists unconsciously determined behavior, automatic, unpremeditated, impulsive, and complex patterns of behavior as examples which have been labeled instinctive by one writer or another.

stincts group their approved instincts into general classes. Thus Colvin and Bagley[1] list 25 instincts under the following general headings: Adaptive, individualistic, sex and parental, social, and religious and esthetic. E. A. Kirkpatrick[2] accepts 30 instincts which he arranges under the following headings: Individualistic or self-preservative, parental, group or social, adaptive, regulative, and resultant or miscellaneous. H. W. Warren[3] has only 26 instincts, which he classifies generally as nutritive, reproductive, defensive, aggressive, and social. Woodworth's 110 instincts are arranged under the three general headings of responses to organic needs, responses to other persons, and play instincts. Watson ("Behavior") has 11 general headings or classes, as follows: 1. Structural characteristics, action systems, etc., 2. obtaining food, 3. shelter, 4. rest, sleep, play, etc., 5. sex, 6. defense and attack, 7. special forms of instinct, 8. vocalization, 9. unclassified and non-adaptive but complex and complete act, 10. unclassified and non-adaptive reflexes, 11. individual peculiarities in response.

Criticism of the current usage of the concept of instinct—Some criticisms of the current usage of the concept of instinct have doubtless already occurred to the reader. One is that there is no sort of agreement in regard to what are the true instincts. Some of the terms, such as acquisition, fighting, sexual love, gregariousness, self-assertion, self-abasement, appear repeatedly in the classifications, but an even larger number of so-called instincts can be found occasionally in a large number of classifications. Sometimes, also, a term which is used as a single specific instinct in one classification may be used to characterize a whole group or class of so-called specific instincts in another classification. An instinct must have original or inherited unity as a behavior pattern or it is not an instinct. A mere group of instincts, a concept, or a classificatory title cannot be an instinct. Such is not a concrete behavior pattern at all, for it does not exist except as a conceptual or abstract meaning term. It

[1] Colvin, S. S. and Bagley, W. C., *Human Behavior: A First Book in Psychology for Teachers.*
[2] Kirkpatrick, E. A., *Fundamentals of Child Study.*
[3] Warren, H. W., *Human Psychology.*

never appears in an adjustment situation as a unitary process of behavior. It is in effect only a list of concrete behavior patterns, which may or may not appear together at any one time or in some one individual organism.

This same criticism applies also to most of the so-called specific instincts in the classifications cited. Thus such terms as fighting, gregariousness, self-assertion, self-abasement, acquisition, play, imitation, and the like are not single and definite behavior patterns. They are class terms for hundreds and thousands of concrete behavior mechanisms which are grouped together in action or in conceptual thinking because of their general similarity of function. There are almost numberless ways of fighting, playing, imitating, or of having gregarious contacts with one's fellows. Each one of these may be a unit behavior pattern and therefore entitled to be called an instinct, if it is inherited. But the whole list of activities having a common conceptual or classificatory name never occur in action together, that is, they never function as a unit behavior process, as would be necessary if they were true instincts. They occur in consciousness only by a short-cut process of symbolic integration and condensation. That is, the whole neuro-muscular organization which would be necessary to the effective overt expression of such a complex so-called instinct does not appear as the basis of the verbal concept which is used to symbolize the group of potential behavior processes included in the reputed instinct. It would probably not be possible for all of such behavior processes to come into consciousness at once in sufficient detail to enable them to go into action. It certainly would not be possible for all of the behavior patterns symbolized by one of these terms, miscalled an instinct, to go into over action at the same time. What we are dealing with in such cases is, therefore, not behavior patterns in the neuro-muscular protoplasmic systems of the organism, but merely a collective or class symbol of many such concrete behavior patterns which never occur together or as a single overt behavior unit. And an instinct must be a unitary behavior pattern or it is not an instinct.

Instincts are structural, not conceptional—An instinct is a biological fact and it is a unit character, or it does not exist. It is structural. It is not possible to inherit an abstraction. The activity, which ordinarily by a species of metonymy is miscalled the instinct, is of course not inherited. The actual instinct which is inherited is the unit organization of the neurons, the physiological and neurological bases of which lie back of and give form to the activity or resulting behavior. The behavior is the visible manifestation of the structural neural organization which is not visible, because it is rooted in an inner neural organization. The behavior is the response of this neuro-muscular organization of the organism to environmental pressures. Only the structural organization can be inherited and therefore be an instinct.

A true classification of the instincts would be a description of these various neural mechanisms. But such a description is of course impossible in the present state of our knowledge about the distribution and organization of neural processes. As a consequence we are compelled to use the less accurate method of classifying instincts in terms of their overt manifestations, that is, in terms of their stimuli and responses. Thorndike* has listed four such methods of classification as follows:

1. By the functions which the tendencies perform
2. By the responses which are their end-terms
3. By the situations which are their first terms
4. By their origins or affinities in development

It is clear of course that there is no relationship of identity between the adjustment-function of a behavior pattern and its structure. The one is a psycho-social fact, is apprehended conceptually, and has objective existence only in consciousness. While the other is a matter of organic relationship and is developed in the protoplasm. Several very diverse structures or behavior patterns may have the same adjustment function, while the same behavior pattern may at different times or in different situations perform antagonistic adjustment functions.

* *Original Nature of Man.*

The structure may be inherited, while the function never can be, since it is organized only conceptually or symbolically as a method of evaluating the adjustment which is made to environment. Neither is there a complete correlation between responses and stimuli, on the one hand, and the behavior patterns or neural organizations, on the other hand, which produce the one and are the result of the other. Consequently these methods of classifying instincts are of but little value.

Examples of conceptual terms mistaken for instincts—Finally, these complex functional or value terms which are miscalled instincts, not only lack the structural unity of instincts, but they are not even inherited units. In each of these complexes of potential activity or behavior represented by such class terms as fighting, the maternal instinct, gregariousness, play, and the like, the acquired elements far outnumber the inherited. Take, for example, the so-called maternal instinct. There is no one activity or set of activities which the instinctivists have in mind when they speak of this "instinct." In different situations and on various occasions the imputed content of this so-called instinct may vary as widely as affection for the child, nursing it, spanking it to make it behave, caressing it, taking it to a baby clinic, getting it off to school, starting it in a profession, and thousands of other things. Of all of the possible activities and attitudes which the mother may manifest toward the child only a few are really inherited, and these are among the simplest of the whole number. They may possibly be represented by such acts as pressing the child to the breast, yielding it milk when it nurses, responding to its presence in the arms by clasping or pressure, and possibly kissing and emotional and mental disturbance when it cries or laughs.

But such acts as these are not sufficient to care for a helpless human infant. The real care of the child, that which enables it to survive and develop into a normal and well adjusted organic and social personality, must be learned. The behavior patterns for such care are acquired by observation and imitation of others in play, by reading books and hearing lectures on the subject, and by the experience of caring for a child. Thus the maternal instinct, which is supposed to account for our behavior in caring for children and to constitute the content of this behavior, turns out to be no instinct at all, is not even a unitary habit process, but is a classificatory concept covering many potential acts which never occur together or in unity. This so-called instinct is an abstract and acquired value term or complex rather than a concrete act. It exists actually as a symbol or as a meaning complex of symbols, but not as overt behavior or action. Consequently it cannot be an instinct. Moreover, the analysis and criticism which have been applied to the term maternal instinct may also be applied with like validity to practically all of the other complex "instincts" in the classifications here cited.

Do instincts exist in man—It may be asked, therefore, if there are any instincts. This question has been raised and sometimes it has been answered in the negative. It seems proper, however, to affirm the existence of instincts, but to deny that they are as numerous or as important relatively in the adjustment processes of man as in the lower animals. As said before, the human instincts which remain intact are concerned primarily with the vegetative or strictly vital processes, rather than with the wider adjustments of the organism to its environment. The latter, and especially those adjustments which we call cultural, are mediated by acquired behavior patterns. If we make a rigid distinction between reflexes and instincts on the basis of the relative complexity of the behavior pattern, then it may be said that there are very few true instincts left intact in the human organism. But there is no definite dividing line between reflexes and instincts on the grounds of complexity, or on any other basis of distinction, and the tendency appears to be to make the term instinct inclusive of that of reflex. From this viewpoint it may be said that we have a great many very simple instincts. But the important fact to note is that the value complexes which for the most part constitute the content of the current classifications of instincts are not instincts, but are acquired complexes and behavior patterns or systems.

3

The Genesis of the Cat's Response to the Rat

ZING YANG KUO

This selection originally appeared in the *Journal of Comparative Psychology*, Vol. 11, 1930, pp. 30-35. It is the summary of a long article in which Kuo describes in careful detail the conditions of several experiments. The summary was chosen because it recapitulates these conditions, and contains his chief views on the subject.

1. The main purposes of this investigation were to determine the effects of the following conditions on the behavior of the kitten toward the rat:

   a. Raising kittens in isolation.
   b. Raising kittens in a rat-killing environment.
   c. Raising kittens in the same cage with rats.
   d. Difference in food-habit, i.e., vegetarianism vs. non-vegetarianism.
   e. Hunger condition, i.e., testing immediately after feeding vs. testing 12 hours after feeding.
   f. Using re-enforcing stimuli, such as seeing the action of rat-killing by another cat to train kittens to kill rats.
   g. Using different kinds of rats, i.e., albino rat, wild gray rat and dancing mouse, to test the preferential responses of the cat to them.
   h. Training the cat to fear the rat, i.e., to run away from the rat by the method of conditioned reflex.

2. Of the 21 kittens raised in the rat-killing environment 18 or more than 85 per cent killed one or more kind of rats before four months old. The kittens always

killed the kind of rat which they saw their mothers kill though they might kill other kinds of rats as well.

3. Of the 20 kittens raised in isolation only 9 (or 45 per cent) killed rats without the so-called learning.

4. All kittens raised in the same cages with rats never killed their cage-mates, though 3 out of 18 killed other kinds of rats.

5. Of 11 non-rat-killing kittens 9 became rat-killers after seeing other cats in the act of killing rats. But with the exception of one kitten the re-enforcing stimulus of seeing other cats killing rats had failed to make the kittens raised in the same cage with rats follow the same action.

6. Vegetarianism had no effect on rat-killing, but had effect on rat-eating.

7. Within the limit of our experiment, hunger condition appears not to have any effect either on rat-eating or on rat-killing.

8. It required an older and larger kitten to kill bigger rats.

9. Kittens that kill large-sized rats will kill small rats of different species also.

10. Environmental influence has a great deal to do with what kind of rat the kitten preferred to kill.

11. The behavior of the kittens to rats was classified into 6 types: (1) positive, (2) negative, (3) oriented, (4) tolerant, (5) playful, (6) hostile.

12. Of these types, type 6 was found to be closely related with type 1, while types 2 and 4 were dominant in the behavior of the non-rat-killing kittens.

13. Our results seem to indicate that larger-sized rats are more likely than smaller ones to call forth hostile and negative responses from kittens, while small-sized rats will more readily call forth killing and playful responses.

14. (1) Types, 2, 3, and 5 for the kittens raised in isolation, (2) type 6 for kittens raised in the rat-killing environment, and (3) type 4 for those raised in the same cage with rats had the largest percentages.

15. The responses of the kittens to the rats which were their cage-mates were classified into the following

types: (1) negative, (2) tolerant, (3) playful, (4) protective, and (5) attaching.

16. We succeeded by the conditioned reflex method in training 3 cats to run away from the rat.

XV. DISCUSSION

In reviewing the results of this study, one is impressed with the fact that the behavior of the cat toward the rat is much more complex and much more variable than most psychologists would have thought. Shall we explain such complexity and variability of the cat's behavior in terms of instinct or in terms of learning? I do not think that these concepts are adequate to describe the responses of the cat to the rat. Nor do we need any such concepts. We have presented the actual behavior picture of the cat towards the rat in terms of stimulus and response together with the life history of the cat. Do we need to add that such responses are instinctive, such and such are learned by trial and error, and such and such are due to insight or ideation? Do we need to add that in our findings the cat shows instincts of rat-killing and rat-eating as well as the instinct to love the rat? Do we need to resort to such concepts as modification of instinct, periodicity of instinct, waning of instinct and the like in order to explain the results of our study?

The cat is a small-sized tiger. Its bodily make-up is especially fitted for capturing small animals; its body and legs are fitted for swift movements, its sharp paws and teeth are fitted for capturing and devouring; and its eyes and ears too, are very helpful in guiding its capturing responses. Here we have a machine so manufactured that under ordinary circumstances it will kill or even eat animals smaller than itself, such as rats, birds, etc. But its swift bodily make-up may also make it playful in response to small animals or small objects especially moving objects. Is it necessary to add that this machine has been endowed by heredity, through its nervous system with the instinct to kill rats and other small animals, and also another instinct to play with them? Should this machine become as large as a tiger, it may even ignore smaller animals such as rats, etc., but will seek to kill much larger ones including men. Shall we say then, that this larger machine possesses an instinct to kill man, and another instinct to pity and forgive rats and other smaller animals? To me, the organismic pattern (please note that I do not mean neural pattern!) or bodily make-up and the size should be sufficient to tell why the cat behaves like cat, the tiger like tiger or the monkey like monkey. The cat has a cat-body and hence the rat-killing behavior; the tiger has a tiger-body and hence man-killing behavior. The chimpanzee has a chimpanzee body, and so uses sticks and does many things almost human. Have the cat and the tiger any instincts? Does the chimpanzee possess any insight? Is the cat's behavior toward the rat hereditary or learned through trial and error, or by imitation? To me, all such questions are useless as well as meaningless (see [2], [3], and [4]).

But the cat is a living machine; it grows and changes; it has a life history. Its behavior is being modified from the moment of fertilization to the point of death, and is modified according to the resultant forces of environmental stimulation, intra-organic as well as extra-organic. In other words, the kinds and range of potential responses of an organism are determined by its bodily size, and especially its bodily make-up or organismic pattern, while its actual responses are determined by its life history. Given an organismic pattern, its behavior can be modified at will by manipulating its life conditions. The function of the behaviorists is to discover the possible kinds and range of activities a given species can perform and to study ways and means to manipulate its responses at will. The ultimate purpose of the science of behavior—and of all other sciences—is "prediction." And accuracy of behavior prediction depends on careful control and careful analysis of physiological factors, life conditions and momentary stimulations. The behaviorist refuses to have anything to do with such verbal labels as instinct, trial and error, insight, "gestalt," purpose and the like, for such concepts are lazy substitutes for careful and detailed analysis of behavior.

The present study does not claim to have achieved the

ideal of accuracy of prediction of behavior. In the first place, the work is still in its rough stage. Secondly, we have not touched upon the physiological side of the responses under investigation. Thirdly, we have not used enough cats to make our results reliable. And finally, we have not studied the behavior of cats toward birds and other small animals, which is so closely related to its behavior toward the rat that reliable knowledge of prediction could only be gained by studying both kinds of behavior. We hope that we shall be able in the near future to publish some more refined work on the cat's behavior toward the rat and other small animals. But the present study, rough as it is, should be sufficient to call attention to the fact that all the experimental investigations in the past in connection with the so-called unlearnedness of instincts, trial and error learning, imitation, insight or gestalt have been so superficial that the more fundamental aspects of behavior have been missed. Is there any wonder, then, that in spite of the fact that more than a quarter of a century has been spent in animal researches, so little has been done towards formulating laws for the prediction of behavior?

The point I am here making is that the mere proof or disproof of an instinct, i.e., action which can be performed without learning, the mere experiments on trial and error learning and the mere test to show the presence or absence of insight or intelligence and imitation will not lead us anywhere. We need to know the potential range or repertory of activities of a given species. We need to know the physiological and genetic or developmental aspects of each behavior. The behavior of an organism is a *passive* affair. How an animal or man will behave in a given moment depends on how it has been brought up and how it is stimulated. Without sufficient knowledge of the physiology of behavior and of the behavior history of the organism, prediction would be impossible. Our study has shown that kittens can be made to kill a rat, to love it, to hate it, to fear it or to play with it: it depends on the life history of the kitten. In the future with more refined methods, with more thorough investigation in this direction and with more knowledge of the physiology of the cat's behavior, we should be able to predict in mathematical terms how a given cat will react to a given rat at a given moment. Prediction of behavior implies knowledge of behavior range, behavior physiology and behavior history. And behavior research means testing the ability of the experimenter to force the organism to behave in the way he desires with minimum energy, effect and time. Our behavior researches in the past have been in the wrong direction, because *instead of finding how we could build nature into the animal, we have tried to find nature in the animal.* Nothing is more natural than for the cat to "love" the rat. And if one insists that the cat has an instinct to kill the rat, I must add that it has an instinct to love the rat too. In behavior nature is what can be built in and not what is supposed to unfold from within. The science of behavior is the science of building nature into animals and men by the most economic methods available (of course, "nature" can be built in only within the potential limit of the organismic pattern). But so far our experimental researches have not been directed toward this goal.

REFERENCES

1. Berry, C. C.: An experimental study of imitation in cats. *Jour. Comp. Neur. and Psych.*, 1908, XVIII, 1-25.
2. Kuo, Z. Y.: A psychology without heredity. *Psychol. Rev.*, 1924, XXXI, 427-448.
3. Kuo, Z. Y.: The fundamental error of the concept of purpose and the trial and error fallacy. *Psychol. Rev.*, 1928, XXXV, 414-433.
4. Kuo, Z. Y.: The net result of the anti-heredity movement in psychology, *Psychol. Rev.*, 1929, XXXVI, 181-200.
5. McDougall, Wm. and McDougall, K. D.: Notes on instinct and intelligence in rats and cats. *Jour. Comp. Psychol.*, 1927, VII, 145-177.

6. Rogers, W. W.: An experimental study of the behavior of kittens toward white albino rats. *Psychol. Bull.*, 1928, XXV, 476-478.
7. Watson, J. B.: *Behavior*, Henry Holt, New York, 1914, Chap. 4.
8. Yerkes, R. M. and Bloomfield, D.: Do kittens instinctively kill mice? *Psychol. Bull.*, 1910, VII, 253-263.

4

Further Study on the Behavior of the Cat Towards the Rat

ZING YANG KUO

This selection originally appeared in The *Journal of Comparative Psychology*, Vol. 25, 1933, pp. 1-8. The experiments described in this paper were originally performed at the National University of Chekiang, Hangchow, China.

INTRODUCTION

In a previous communication which was published in this JOURNAL some years ago (Kuo, '30), the results of a series of experiments to determine the effects of different environmental conditions on the behavior of the kitten toward rats and mice were reported. The results showed, among other things, that if a kitten was raised in the same cage with a rat since it was very young, it, when grown up, became tolerant of rats: not only would it never attack a rat, but it adopted the rat as its "mate," played with it, and even became attached to it. Even frequent observation of killing and eating of rats by other cats could not induce such a kitten to change the type of reaction toward the rat which it had acquired in its early post-natal life.

In the experiment which is to be reported below, the condition was modified so that the new born kitten lived not only with rats in the same cage but also with two or three other kittens. The purpose was to find out whether the kitten, living under such changed conditions, would behave toward its rat mates differently from the type of responses found in the kitten which was raised alone in the same cage with a single rat as reported in the previous article.

In addition, we shall include in this report the result of another experiment in which kittens were kept in the same cage with sparrows since they were young.

EXPERIMENT I

Methods

This experiment deals with the behavior of kittens raised in the same cage with rats. There were 17 kittens used in this experiment. They were divided into four groups, three groups having four kittens each, and one having five. Kittens in each group were of the same litter. Soon after the kittens were born, they were kept together (without their mother) in a cage in which a pair of albino rats, one male and one female, were living. At the time the kittens were introduced into the rats' cage, the latter were about one month old. Neither gray mice nor dancing mice were used in this experiment. Other conditions of the experiment were the same as those reported in the former paper.

The kittens were separated from the rats after nine months. One month after separation, each kitten was tested for its reaction to the adult albino rat. The test was made once a month for four months. The rats used for such tests were the kitten's original cage mates. But in some cases in which the original mates had been killed or died, substitutes of approximately the same size and same age were employed.

Four and a half months after separation those cats which were still indifferent to the presence of the albino rat were tested for imitation of rat killing response. The procedure of the imitation test will be described in its proper place.

Results

The results of this experiment may be briefly stated as follows:

1. During those nine months' stay with two rats in the same cage all the kittens were indifferent and tolerant with reference to the rats. They let the rats run about in the cage, climb over their back or head and eat with them in the same dish. Many of the kittens would let the rats pull a piece of meat or fish away from their mouth. Seven kittens of seventeen made attempts to play with the rats.

2. None of the kittens were attached to a rat as was the case in the previous experiment in which only one kitten was kept in the same cage with a single rat. The separation of the rats from the cage at any period and for any length of time did not cause any "seeking" or "restless" movements. Nor did the returning of the rats to the cage change the behavior of the kittens. Not a single kitten ever showed any response which might be regarded as protection for the rat. All such reactions are quite a contrast to those found in the kitten which was kept alone in the same cage with only one rat. In the latter case the kitten was generally attached to the rat. To quote from the former report. "After the cage-mate—the rat—was taken from the cage, the kitten began to mew continuously, became restless and searched from corner to corner until the rat was returned to the cage." The kittens of the present experiment never exhibited such kind of responses with reference to the rat.

However, every kitten was attached to its own sisters and brothers in the cage; they played, ate, and slept together. If one of the kittens was left alone in the cage, it became restless and mewed until at least one of them was returned. The presence of the two albino rats in the cage did not alter the restless movements of the kitten, "seeking" for its missing sisters and brothers.

3. The behavior of the rats in the cage toward the kittens was also a sort of indifference. They played with each other, ran about, performed sex act, built nests, gave birth to young rats, and nursed them, as if the kittens were not present in the cage. They ate together with the kittens from the same dish and would sometimes try to pull a piece of meat or fish from the mouth of a kitten, as has been stated before. When some of the

female rats were pregnant or nursing the young, they became very spirited and would attack kittens if they came near their nest. The kitten then became afraid of these rats and would not dare approach their nests.

4. The behavior of the kittens toward the new born rats in the cage was striking. Twelve out of the seventeen kittens killed and ate new born rats whenever they happened to come to the rats' nest. This was always done in the absence of the mother rat from the nest. If the mother was in the nest, the kittens kept away from it. The young rats were stolen from the nest and killed and eaten in some other place in the cage. In many cases the mother rat saw the kittens eat her young in a corner of the cage without making any effort to interfere with them as long as they were not near her nest. Some of the mother rats would, however, carry the dead bodies of the young rats back to the nests after they were killed and left alone without being eaten by the kittens. Others would join the kittens and share with them the meat of their own young.

The kittens began to steal and eat new born rats when they were from two to four months old. Once they tasted the meat of young rats, they would repeat the same act each time the mother rat gave birth to a new litter. One group ate as many as five litters during their nine months stay with the rats. The behavior of the kittens toward the adult rats remained the same as before even after they had eaten several litters of their offspring.

5. In view of the fact that the kittens killed and ate new born rats without changing their original behavior toward the adult rats, tests were made to find out whether their reactions to the rats not living together with them in the same cage would be the same as those to the young rats. As the kittens always killed and ate young rats before hair grew on their body, the test rats were divided into two groups: in one the fur was completely shaved, while in the other the hair of the rat was kept intact. The ages of the test rats in the two groups were the same: one day old, one week, two weeks, one month, two months, and three months old. The tests were made when the kittens were about five months old. The kittens

were tested separately. One test was given every other day. In each test one shaved and one unshaved rat were used. They were of the same age. The unshaved rat was introduced to the kitten first. The shaved rat was put in after the unshaved one was taken out.

The result is noteworthy. Eleven of the twelve kittens which killed new born rats before invariably killed and ate hairless or shaved rats, regardless of the differences in the age of the test rats. But their reactions to the unshaved rats were the same as those to the adult rats living in the same cage with them.

Only one of those five kittens which did not kill new born rats killed two shaved rats, one of which was one month old and the other two months old.

6. The result of the tests of the kittens' behavior toward their former cage-mates—the adult rats—from whom the kittens had been separated for from one to four months was negative for sixteen cats. Throughout the four tests made during the four months of separation these kittens remained indifferent to the presence of the rats although they continued to kill and eat new born and shaved rats.

The only exception was found in one cat which killed one male rat—its original cage-mate—in the fourth test, that is, the test four months after the separation.

7. After these sixteen cats were found to still remain indifferent to the adult white rats even after four and a half months of separation, tests for imitation were initiated. The tests consisted of letting each of these cats see through, in the same cage, the performance of killing and eating rats by another cat. The rat was first put before the cat in the cage under test. If it failed to attack the rat, a rat-killing cat was added to the cage. After the killing act was performed, the killer was taken out and another rat of approximately the same size was put before the would-be imitator whose reactions to the rat were recorded. This procedure was repeated every day for two weeks or until the act of imitation was observed.

The result of the imitation test was also striking. Of the sixteen cats tested, six attempted, after several times seeing killing and eating of rats by other cats, to attack rats which were their former cage-mates. But only three of these six cats succeeded in killing rats. The other three would not dare to approach a rat again after they were once bitten back by the rat in their first attempt to attack it. These three cats, however, would carry in their mouths a dead rat killed by some other cat, and growl, hiss and play with it. But the dead rat was finally given up without being eaten. All the six cats mentioned in this paragraph killed and ate new born and shaved rats before they were separated from the adult rats with which they lived together for nine months.

EXPERIMENT II

Methods

In this experiment the purpose was to test the reaction of young kittens to sparrows which were kept in the same cage. Nine kittens from three litters were used. They were divided into three groups. Before their eyes were open each group of kittens was placed in a cage in which four to five adult sparrows had been kept. At first the sparrows were frightened by the introduction of the kittens into the cage, but after from one to three days all of them became adapted to the new situation. In this way the kittens and sparrows were kept together for six months. The behavior of the kittens in the same cage, especially with reference to the sparrows, was observed and recorded from day to day.

Results

The results of this experiment may be summarized as follows:

All of the nine kittens paid no attention to the sparrows in the cage for the first two months. Their behavior toward the sparrow is almost the same as that of the kittens toward white rats in experiment I. But when they were a little over two months old, five of the kittens began to follow the sparrows in their flight in the cage. As soon as the flight ceased, the pursuit of the kittens subsided. But some of the sparrows became frightened by the pursuit of the kittens and flew in panic. This made the pursuit of the kittens more active and zealous. Three kittens on different occasions happened to each catch one sparrow during flight. One of these kittens (No. 6) later developed a habit of capturing sparrows in flight and playing with them without any attempt to kill them. The other two (Nos. 4 and 7) did exactly the same for the first five to ten days, but later on they killed and devoured the sparrow soon after it was caught in flight. It must be noted in passing that other kittens did not "imitate" the actions of kittens 4, 6, and 7.

After six months all the nine kittens were separated from their birdmates and set free but their reactions to sparrows and other small birds were watched in the garden and elsewhere for two months. Except Nos. 4, 6, and 7, none of the kittens was ever observed to pay attention to sparrows or other small birds. But No. 6 often made attempts to capture sparrows or small birds without success. After five days its interest in sparrows and other small birds seemed to have waned. On the other hand, Nos. 4 and 7 continued to capture and eat sparrows and other small birds as they did when they were kept in the cage. These two kittens were seen also to catch and eat frogs and wild mice.

DISCUSSION

The results of these two experiments seem to further demonstrate the view held by the writer many years ago, that other things being equal the behavior of the animal is determined by its early environment in which it is raised. Kittens raised in a "rat-killing environment" are most likely to be "rat-killers"; raised in isolation, the probability of rat-killing is almost fifty-fifty (Kuo, '30). But when one kitten is raised *alone* with one rat in the same cage, it became attached to the rat, and would never attack it, even after having seen through many times the act of killing rats by other cats (Kuo, '30). On the other hand, if more than one kitten is raised in the same cage with the rat, it develops no attachment to the rat. Instead, its attachment is for its brother or sister kittens. Furthermore, there is a high possibility that after long separation from the rats, these kittens may develop a habit of killing rats either spontaneously or through imitation, as we have seen in experiment I. Such a possibility is almost nil in the case in which only one new born kitten is raised in the same cage with one rat.

Again, while the writer is not as yet able to ascertain the factors which influence the kittens to eat the newly born rats, the fact that they kill and eat shaved rats and pay no attention to unshaved ones points to the same conclusion, namely, that the action of eating shaved rats is a carryover from their early behavior in eating new born rats. The results of experiment II also demonstrate the effects of early behavior which is a direct result of environmental conditions, and its carryover and transfer in later life.

In the case of the chick, the writer has given numerous evidences to show the effects of embryonic behavior upon its life after hatch (Kuo, '32). It cannot be overemphasized that ontogeny, or the developmental study of behavior is one of the most important channels through which causal factors of behavior may be discovered.

REFERENCES

1. Kuo, Z. Y. 1930. The genesis of the cat's behavior toward the rat. *Jour. Comp. Psychol.*, 11, 1-35.
2. Kuo, Z. Y. 1932. Ontogeny of embryonic behavior in aves. IV. The influence of prenatal behavior upon postnatal life. *Jour. Comp. Psychol.*, 14, 109-121.
3. Kuo, Z. Y. 1937. Prolegomena to Praxiology. *Jour. Psychol.*, 4, 1-22.
4. Rogers, W. W. 1932. Controlled observation on the behavior of kittens toward the rat from birth to five months of age. *Jour. Comp. Psychol.*, 13, 107-125.

5

The Development of Behavior in Vertebrates Experimentally Removed from the Influence of External Stimulation

LEONARD CARMICHAEL

This article originally appeared in the *Psychology Review*, 1927, 34, pp. 34-47.

In a previous paper [1] certain preliminary results were presented which were derived from an experimental study of the development of organisms artificially removed from the influence of external stimulation. Criticisms of this paper which have been kindly offered have shown that the facts there presented were not readily comprehended in their full systematic setting. In an effort to make the setting of the problem more clear, therefore, the present paper is divided into three sections: (I) A presentation of the current status of the problem of the development of behavior and a criticism of relevant experimental work. (II) A report of the results of a new series of experiments. (III) A theoretical evaluation of the significance of the findings reported.

PART I
HISTORICAL AND CRITICAL

As typical of the pioneer experimental work aimed to determine that which is native and that which is inherited in behavior may be taken the investigations of D. A. Spalding [2]. In his studies Spalding carried on a number of experiments, one of which was the hooding of chicks just as they came from the shell. The birds were kept thus blinded for several days. The hoods were then withdrawn and the initial pecking reaction noted. The accuracy of the chicks on being thus released was 'marvelous at the very beginning' [3]. He noted, nevertheless, that "most frequently, however, they struck five or six times, lifting the head once or twice before they succeeded in swallowing the first food" [4]. Spalding also studied other birds and certain mammals. For example, he confined recently-hatched swallows in a small box in such a manner that they could not fly. At an age when similar birds were flying the individuals of the experimental group were liberated. The birds flew off at the first trial but their flight was not absolutely perfect. Certainly, too, in the box in which they developed they could have gained much wing exercise [5]. This work of Spalding has been very widely quoted [6]. At least by the earlier writers it was often extravagantly praised. James characterizes it as 'wonderful' and Romanes says, "Spalding in his brilliant researches on this subject has not only placed beyond all question the falsity of the view 'that all the supposed examples of instinct may be nothing more than cases of rapid learning, imitation and instruction,' but also proved that a young bird or mammal comes into the world with an amount and nicety of ancestral knowledge that is highly astonishing" [7].

That these experiments of Spalding did not 'put beyond all question' the view that behavior is individually acquired is shown by the results of later and much more carefully controlled experiments. Breed, and later Shepard and Breed [8], have shown that the chicks' initial accuracy of pecking, proclaimed and emphasized by Spalding, is not verifiable. Craig has also shown that certain birds must learn to drink [9]. Many other objections to Spalding's results have been raised. Most significant in refutation of the claim that Spalding's experiment settled once and for all time the question of the relationship between heredity and environment is the fact stated tersely by Breed that "the early post-embryonic life of the chicks continued the scope and activities already begun in the egg" [10]. Strangely enough Spalding himself knew of this objection, but he waives it aside. He quotes and adversely criticizes the following statement made by

Helmholtz, which might well have been made by a modern 'anti-instinct' psychologist. "The young chicken very soon pecks at grains of corn, but it pecked while it was still in the shell, and when it hears the hen peck it pecks again, at first seemingly at random. Then when it has by chance hit upon a grain it may, no doubt, learn to notice the field of vision which is at that moment presented to it" [11].

It is this very fact, which cannot, indeed, be emphasized too strongly, namely, that behavior does begin before birth or hatching, that makes the major contentions of these experiments invalid [12].

Even the carefully controlled experiments of Breed and of Breed and Shepard while demonstrating many important facts in regard to development are also open to this objection. A bird that is hatched or an animal that is born is already environmentally conditioned [13]. Moseley's experiments upon similar material are even less calculated to determine the relative parts of heredity and environment in determining the initial performance of the actions which are later called pecking. In her experiments the chicks which were studied were given ample opportunity for exercise save that they were kept in the dark [14].

Bird, another recent student of this subject, on the contrary, notes that the increase in the pecking 'instinct,' shown graphically in so many studies, may not be the specific maturation of any specific synaptic connections. He shows that the early 'maturation' of pecking may be but a 'general improvement in motor control' [15]. Moreover, this same experimentalist holds that after this initial period "practice and habit formation are adequate explanatory concepts of the perfection of the swallowing reactions of the chick" [16]. In a later paper, however, Bird makes it very clear that his observations on the initial specificity of the behavior of young chicks make him far from a supporter of Kuo's contention that the conditioning of the post-natal environment is a sufficient explanation of the origin of behavior patterns [17].

Obviously, the complicated activity of the bird in liberating itself from the egg cannot be ignored [18]. Even this behavior, however, is really an advanced stage in the embryonic activity of the organism [19]. Elsewhere I have attempted to show that there is no theoretical compulsion to believe that even the very early actions of the embryo in the egg or in the uterus are purely native [20].

While valuable in other respects, the conclusions of Yerkes on the heredity of savageness and wildness in rats, and of Yerkes and Bloomfield on the hunting activities of kittens do not show that the specific motor acts noted occurred for the first time in the behavior observed [21]. Indeed, as these latter writers admit, 'racial and individual experience' early become so 'completely intermingled' that separation is, to say the least, difficult [22].

The studies of the development of sex behavior are significant, also, rather as an example of the integration of elementary acts into a complex and comparatively unitary behavior pattern than as a demonstration of the native origin of the part-acts themselves [23]. The 'abnormalities' of the sex function discovered in animals raised under peculiar conditions show the essential part played by the environment in the development of these activities [24].

The great difficulty, moreover, of pointing to any satisfactory criterion of the innate is another factor that has led to the partial or absolute rejection of the concept of heredity as a determiner of conduct [25].

Even McDougall admits that from the standpoint of what he terms 'the mechanistic hypothesis' the conception of inherited behavior must be rejected. He holds that instinct, for example, cannot intelligibly be held to consist of more or less compound reflex action. The motor mechanisms employed in instinctive acts, he avers, are, at least in some measure, made up of responses that have been individually acquired and previously practiced [26].

This criticism is one that must be heeded by the scientific student who accepts the mechanistic principle as a working hypothesis. If an act is to be declared *hereditary* it must be shown to occur for the first time in a manner that is independent of environmental conditioning.

It is to meet this challenge that the present series of experiments were devised. In the experiments already reported, as well as in certain earlier work by previous investigators there cited, it is shown that it is possible to allow organisms to develop under an anaesthetic such that morphological growth occurs in the absolute absence of observable external movements. Such organisms are allowed to grow, so that externally they appear better developed than a similar group of normal organisms when they began swimming. At this stage the experimental animals are released from the anaesthetic in which they have developed. Thus, after a period of complete inactivity, the experimenter can record the time necessary for the very first response to develop in the organisms. This time is shown to be surprisingly short.

What process is occurring during the short period after the organism is removed from the anaesthetic and before it makes any observable response to the continual external stimulation to which it is subjected? Is this a period of rapid neutral change? Is it a period of exceedingly rapid learning? Or, is it merely a period of time necessary to remove the masking effect of the anaesthetic? If answers can be given to these questions it will be possible to state with some assurance whether or not 'preformed pathways' exist which are ready to function before they have been exercised. Even, however, if it is demonstrated that such pathways do exist it will by no means be equivalent to saying that these pathways are the result of the mere innate maturation of certain germinal determiners and that they have come into existence in independence of the environment. An alternative and seemingly more satisfactory position than this will be considered in the last section of the present paper.

PART II
EXPERIMENTAL

Unlike the previous series of experiments in which the embryos of both the frog (Rana sylvatica) and the salamander (Amblystoma punctatum) were employed, in the present series only amblystoma were used. This selection was made because of the size of the organisms and because previous trials had shown them to respond satisfactorily to an anaesthetic. This type, moreover, is rendered peculiarly available because of the fact that its embryological development has been most thoroughly studied. Coghill has made remarkable and detailed experimental studies of many phases both of the anatomical and physiological development of this organism [27].

The eggs used in the present series of experiments were secured in the same locality previously reported and the technique of preparation was the same as that already described.

At a period of morphological development well previous to the point at which any apparent movement occurs, the organisms were placed in individual glass development dishes. These dishes were then divided into two groups. One set, the *control group*, was filled with tap water while the other, the *experimental group*, was filled with an anaesthetic solution of the desired strength. Chloretone was again used as the anaesthetic. The typical strength of the solution, save where it was varied as noted below, was four parts of chloretone in 10,000 parts of water.

The experimental work was carried on in a room which maintained as nearly as possible an even temperature. No especial effort, however, was made to regulate either this factor or the light in the room as both the experimental animals and the control group were at all times subject to the same conditions. The development of the drugged and the normal embryos as judged by external appearance was quite similar. In all cases, however, development seemed to be somewhat more slow in the anaesthetized group. Possibly because of improved ability on the part of the experimenter in removing the protective 'jelly' of the eggs, fewer abnormal individuals developed in this series of experiments than in those previously reported.

Soon after the larvae in the control dishes began to respond to the stimulation of a light touch with a blunt rod, they became free swimmers. The drugged embryos during this period showed absolutely no response to stimulation, nor in any case did they respond before they were released from the anaesthetic.

When the drugged organism showed a morphological development in advance of that shown by the individuals of the control group when they had first become good swimmers, the drugged organisms were released. This release was accomplished by removing the organisms one by one from the anaesthetic bath and placing them in tap water. As soon as they were placed in the fresh water they were subjected to continual gentle stimulation and the time was taken from the moment of immersion in the tap water until the first movement occurred. This time for the first series of the present experiment is shown in the second line of Table I.

TABLE I

Showing time elapsing after removing embryos from the anaesthetic solution in which they had developed before the first response to stimulation was noted

Embryo number	1	2	3	4	5	6	7	8	9	10	11	12	13	14	15	16	17	18
Time in minutes	4	4	3	6	5	5	4	2	2	4	5	4	7	3	5	5	4	5

After all of these experimental animals had been released a period of 36 hours was allowed to elapse during which the members of the experimental group normally swam about in tap water. When this period had passed, the same individuals (they were at all times kept distinct in numbered dishes) were re-anaesthetized in a solution of the same concentration in which they had developed. The time required for observable response to stimulation to cease after re-immersion in the drug solution is shown in the second line of Table II.

The organisms were allowed to stay in this solution once again in a condition of apparently complete inactivity for twenty-four hours. At the conclusion of this period they were individually removed from the drug

TABLE II

Showing time in minutes required for re-anaesthetizing embryos noted in Table I and time elapsing after they were removed from the anaesthetic the second time and before the second response was observed

Embryo number	1	2	3	4	5	6	7	8	9	10	11	12	13	14	15	16	17	18
Time required for re-anaesthetizing	1	3	1	2	2	3	1	2	2	1	1	2	3	1	1	1	2	2
Time to emerge from second anaesthetic	5	4	6	5	5	5	3	4	5	5	3	4	8	4	4	6	6	6

and placed in tap water. The time required after this second immersion in fresh water for response to occur is shown in line three of Table II.

In Table III are shown the results of a check experi-

TABLE III

Showing the time in minutes required for anaesthetizing normal embryos raised to free swimming stage in fresh water. Also showing time required for first response to occur after their removal from anaesthetic

Embryo number	19	20	21	22	23	24	25	26
Time for anaesthesia	2	1	2	2	2	2	2	1
Time for elimination of anaesthetic	7	8	11	8	6	8	10	8

ment in which certain of the organisms of the control group which had developed normally in tap water were anaesthetized after they had been free swimmers for several days.

In order to determine if possible the role of the anaesthetic in determining the time required for arousal from narcosis certain individuals were placed in chloretone solutions of varying strengths. For the most part these experiments were failures. The increased strength of the drug killed the organisms. A few, however, of the free swimming larvae place in a solution of 8 parts of chloretone in 10,000 parts of water developed in such a manner that the time required for the release could be taken. The times required for the complete anaesthesis (as shown by the cessation of response to external stimulation) and for subsequent arousal are shown in Table IV.

TABLE IV

Time required in minutes for inducing anaesthesia and subsequent arousal in previously free-swimming organisms placed in a strong anaesthetic solution of 8 parts chloretone in 10,000 parts of water

Embryo number	27	28	29	30
Time to induce anaesthetic state	.5	.5	.4	.2
Time for release	30	10	18	33

The conclusion of the present experiments is that there is little significant difference in the time required for the very first observable response on release for the anaesthetic in an organism that has never before shown movement and in one that has been free moving, re-anaesthetized, and released the second time. This evidence together with that shown in Table IV seems to point to the nature of the process that occurs between the time of the immersion of the anaesthetized organism in fresh water and its first movement. This process appears to be no more rapid than is the elimination of the masking effect of the anaesthetic upon organisms which already have well integrated response mechanisms. It may, therefore, safely be assumed that the time required for release is not a period of learning but rather an interval required for the removal of the masking effect of the anaesthetic.

PART III
THEORETICAL

At first sight these results, therefore, seem to give confirmation to the hypothesis that the neuromuscular mechanism upon which behavior depends is developed in the individual by a mere maturation of innate determiners. This view is commonly held by a number of physiological psychologists [28]. The results presented here are not conclusive enough, the present writer believes, to merit the acceptance of the radical form of the maturation hypothesis. It seems true, however, that the findings of the present experiments give better evidence for this view than has at times been taken as completely satisfactory by the nativistic psychologists.

The question may then be asked: If the reflex mechanism upon which the first response of amblystoma depend are not developed by mere maturation, how is it that they are ready to function the first time they are effectively stimulated in an organism that has just been released from an anaesthetic in which it has developed from an early and immobile stage?

Before this question may specifically be solved for the particular type under consideration it may be well to consider in outline the general status of the problem of development. An answer, indeed, to this question may only be given by a study of the dynamic process of embryological development. One who accepts the strict maturation view must show how, *by heredity alone,* such hypothetical entities as Thorndike's 'performed bonds' of the germ cell become the real neural connections determining the behavior of the adult. The biologists who are interested in heredity, have displayed far too little interest, as Pearl has shown, in this all important process of somatogenesis [29]. The criticism may be urged with even greater force against the nativistic psychologists for these writers have almost completely ignored the developmental embryology of the structures that they posit as the basis of innate behavior. And yet, if *maturation* is to be more than a vitalistic shibboleth, the process by which it occurs must at least be suggested. Otherwise the growth of the neuromuscular mechanisms upon which native behavior is supposed to depend must seem to result from some bold necromancy comparable to the erection of the pleasure palaces of Eastern romance which only become a theatre of activity after their magical construction.

Those familiar only with biological literature, and who have not studied the writings of the nativistic psychologists may think that the present criticism is an attack upon a man of straw. There can be no doubt, however, as I have shown elsewhere [30], that unmitigated preformism still permeates much psychological writing. This view certainly must be modified for as Professor Jennings has recently said: "Or more properly, characteristics are not inherited at all; what one inherits is certain material that under certain conditions will produce a particular characteristic; if those characteristics are not supplied, some other characteristic is produced" [31].

The suggestion has been made that the term *heredity* be held to include the normal environmental influence, but to the present writer this seems like solving a very genuine physiological problem by a verbal trick [32].

If the hypothesis that the organism is equipped with certain preformed structures, which develop without the aid of the environment be rejected, it seems equally true that the contention that all behavior may be explained as the result of post-natal conditioning is equally in error. Strangely enough, however, there are psychologists, such as Kuo, who make this assertion [33]. The whole gradual process of building up behavior patterns in pre-natal life to which reference is made in the early part of this paper is sufficient evidence against this view.

Beside these two radical views of psychological preformism and psychological epigenesis there is of course a middle view which the present writer has defended in the past and which it seems must implicitly be held by most students of this problem. This hypothesis holds that *all* behavior is the result of the *interdependent*, but not necessarily equal activity of certain factors which may be classed as hereditary and those factors which may be classed as environmental. According to this view the intricate development of receptors, nerve trunks, central apparatus, and motor end-organs appears, not as a teleological preparation for the future, but as the result of the truly mechanistic determination carried out by means of a functional stimulation and response within the organism itself [34].

In the light of the above discussion the specific problem of this paper may now be considered. In the work here reported it is shown that a neuromuscular apparatus that had never before functioned as a response mechanism is capable of determining external behavior the very first time that it is effectively stimulated. To the present writer this seems to point to the fact that this mechanism had been developed by certain processes of a stimulus-response nature within the organism itself [35]. The old view that functional activity is dependent upon myelinization has recently been revived, but this too is still in question [36].

In summary and conclusion it may be said that the experiments reviewed in the first section of the paper do not show what behavior is native and what behavior is acquired. Even the experiments here reported, in which the very first external movements are studied, do not give final evidence upon this question. It has been shown, nevertheless, that the time elapsing after the removal of the organism from the anaesthetic before the first movement occurs is probably the time necessary for the elimination of the narcotic and not a period of functional development. Theoretically it is pointed out that these results seem still to point to the conclusion presented in previous papers, namely, that the development of the behavior mechanism is not alone dependent upon heredity or environment, but that it is the result of the *inter-dependent* action of both of these factors.

REFERENCES

1. CARMICHAEL, L., 'The Development of Behavior in Vertebrates Experimentally Removed from the In-

fluence of External Stimulation,' *Psychol. Rev.*, 1926, 33, pp. 51-58.

2. SPALDING, D. A., 'Instinct with Original Observations on Young Animals,' *Macmillan's Mag.*, 1873, 27, pp. 282-293 (also reprinted in the *Pop. Sci. Mo.*, 1902, 61, pp. 126-142). See, also, *Idem*, 'Instinct and Acquisition,' *Nature*, 1875, 12, pp. 507 f.
3. *Op. cit.* in *Macmillan's Mag.*, p. 284.
4. *Ibid.*, p. 284.
5. *Op. cit.* in *Nature*, p. 507.
6. Among the many who have made reference to Spalding's results may be noted the following:

   PREYER, W., *The Mind of the Child*, Part I, 1890, pp. 336 ff.

   JAMES, W., *Principles of Psychology*, 1890, II, pp. 396 ff.

   ROMANES, G. J., *Mental Evolution in Animals*, 1883, pp. 161-165, 170-171, 175, 213, and 216.

   MORGAN, C. L., *An Introduction to Comparative Psychology*, 1894, pp. 202 and 208.

   Idem, *Animal Life and Intelligence*, 1895, pp. 395 ff.

   MILLS, W., *The Nature and Development of Animal Intelligence*, 1898, p. 261.

   BALDWIN, J. M., *Development and Evolution*, 1902, p. 139.

   HOLMES, S. J., *The Evolution of Animal Intelligence*, 1911, p. 99.

   THORNDIKE, E. L., *Animal Intelligence*, 1911, pp. 163-165.

   BREED, F. S., 'The Development of Certain Instincts and Habits in Chicks,' *Behav. Monog.*, 1911, I, pp. 2 ff.

   SHEPARD, J. F. AND BREED, F. S., 'Maturation and Use in the Development of an Instinct,' *J. Animal Behav.*, 1913, 3, pp. 283 ff.

   WATSON, J. B., *Behavior, An Introduction to Comparative Psychology*, 1914, p. 146.

   HUNTER, W. S., *General Psychology*, 1919, p. 166.

   SMITH, S., AND GUTHRIE, E. R., *General Psychology in Terms of Behavior*, 1921, pp. 139 and 143.

   ALLPORT, F. H., *Social Psychology*, 1924, pp. 44 ff.

7. ROMANES, G. J., *op. cit.*, p. 161.
8. In the articles cited above.
9. CRAIG, W., 'Observations on Doves Learning to Drink,' *J. Animal Behav.*, 1912, 2, pp. 273-279.
10. BREED, F. S., *op. cit.*, p. 75.
11. SPALDING, D. A., *loc. cit.* in *Nature*.
12. For experimental work calculated to throw light upon the prenatal responses of organisms, cf. PREYER, W., *Die Seele des Kindes*, 1884 (translated 1890, pp. 212 ff); MINKOWSKI, M., 'Zum gegenwärtigen Stand der Lehre von den Reflexen,' *Neurologische und psychiatrische Abhandlungen aus dem Sweizer Arch. f. Neur. u. Psychiat.*, 1925, Heft I; LANE, H. H., 'The Correlation between Structure and Function in Development of the Special Senses of the White Rat,' A Dissertation, Norman, Oklahoma, 1917; PATON, S., 'The Reactions of the Vertebrate Embryo and the Associated Changes in the Nervous System,' *Mitt. a. d. Zool. Stat. z. Neap.*, 1907, 18, pp. 535-581; *Idem*, (second paper) *J. Comp. Neur.*, 1911, 21, pp. 345-372; BROWN, T. G., 'On the Activities of the Central Nervous System of the Unborn Foetus of the Cat, with a Discussion of the Question whether Progression (Walking, etc.) Is a 'Learnt' Complex,' *J. Physiol.*, 1915, 49, pp. 208-215. Also the at present unpublished work of AVERY, G. T., AND STONE, C. P., on congenital behavior exhibited by prenatally delivered guinea-pigs.
13. The importance of this conception for human psychology has been made very explicit by J. B. WATSON, *Behaviorism*, 1924, pp. 88 ff.
14. MOSELEY, D., 'The Accuracy of the Pecking Response in Chicks,' *J. Comp. Psychol.*, 1925, 5, pp. 75-97.
15. BIRD, C., 'The Relative Importance of Maturation and Habit in the Development of An Instinct,' *Ped. Sem.*, 1925, 32, p. 81.
16. *Ibid.*, p. 91.
17. *Idem*, 'The Effect of Maturation upon the Pecking Instinct of Chicks,' *Ibid.*, 1926, 33, p. 219.
18. CRAIG, W., 'Behavior of Young Birds in Breaking out

of the Egg,' *J. Animal Behav.*, 1912, 2, pp. 296-298.
19. PATON, S., 'Experiments on Developing Chicken's Eggs,' *J. Exper. Zool.*, 1911, 11, pp. 469-472.
20. CARMICHAEL, L., 'Heredity and Environment: Are they Antithetical?' *J. Abn. & Soc. Psychol.*, 1925, 20, 245-260.
21. YERKES, R. M., 'The Heredity of Savageness and Wildness in Rats,' *J. Animal Behav.*, 1913, 3, pp. 286-296, and YERKES, R. M., AND BLOOMFIELD, D., 'Do Kittens Instinctively Kill Mice?' *Psychol. Bull.*, 1910, 7, pp. 253-263.
22. *Ibid.*, p. 263.
23. Cf. STONE, C. P., 'The Congenital Sexual Behavior of the Young Male Albino Rat,' *J. Comp. Psychol.*, 1922, 2, pp. 95-153, and *Idem*, 'The Awakening of Copulatory Ability in the Male Albino Rat,' *Amer. J. Physiol.*, 1924, 68, pp. 407.
24. For a discussion of the point and references to the experimental literature see ALLPORT, F. H., *Social Psychology*, 1924, pp. 698 ff.
25. For a bibliography of this so-called anti-instinct controversy see my paper, *op. cit.* in the *J. Abn. & Soc. Psychol.*
26. MCDOUGALL, W., 'The Use and Abuse of Instinct in Social Psychology,' *J. Abn. & Soc. Psychol.*, 1921-1922, 16, pp. 310 f. With the alternative vitalistic principle now held by this writer we are not concerned in this paper. He holds that an innate instinct with all its hormic phylogenetic potency may make use of any motor mechanisms however developed and still constitute inherited behavior.
27. For the student of behavior this series of papers is most significant. They range from 1902 to the present. Particular reference should be made to a group of papers on 'Correlated Anatomical and Physiological Studies of the Growth of the Nervous System of Amphibia,' (Nos. I to V) *J. Comp. Neur.*, 1914, 24; *Ibid.*, 1916, 26; *Ibid.*, 1924, 37; *Ibid.*, 1926, 40.
28. W. S. HUNTER says, for example (*General Psychology*, 1919, pp. 166 ff): "Undoubtedly as the chick grows older the nerve centers (synaptic connec-

tions) which control the instinct are maturing so that part of the increase in efficiency is due to the growth of the instinct as a result of strictly inherited tendencies. This has been tested and proven to be the case by Shepard and Breed, 1914." And E. L. Thorndike says (*Educational psychology*, Vol. I, pp. 1 ff): "Any man possesses at the very start of life —that is, at the very moment when the ovum and spermatozoön which are to produce him have united —numerous well defined tendencies to future behavior. Between the situations which he will meet and the responses which he will make to them, preformed bonds exist."

29. PEARL, R., *Modes of Research in Genetics*, 1915, pp. 2 ff.
30. CARMICHAEL, L., loc. cit. in *J. Abn. & Soc. Psychol.*
31. JENNINGS, H. S., *Prometheus*, 1925, p. 43.
32. Cf. WELLS, W. R., "The Meaning of "Inherited" and "Acquired" in Reference to Instinct,' *J. Abn. & Soc. Psychol.*, 1922, 17, pp. 160 ff.
33. KUO, Z. Y., 'A Psychology without Heredity,' *Psycol. Rev.*, 1924, 31, 427-447.
34. This problem has been treated in an original manner that is slightly different from the view presented here by R. M. OGDEN, 'Crossing "The Rubicon Between Mechanism and Life,"' *J. Phil.*, 1925, 22, pp. 281-293.
35. Much is known regarding the nature of these processes, but as yet there is no unanimity of opinion upon them by the students best qualified to judge. Chemical, electrical, and vibratory theories have been advanced to account for the development of an interrelationship of nerve cells. Cf. HERRICK, C. J., *Neurological Foundations of Animal Behavior*, 1924, pp. 111 ff. and the references there cited. See also, WEISS, P., 'The Relations between Central and Peripheral Coordination,' *J. Comp. Neur.*, 1926, 40, pp. 241-251. As I have elsewhere suggested the hypothesis of Bok and Kappers as developed in the conception of neurobiotaxis seems most satisfactory. This view in any event scarcely merits the curt dis-

missal which it receives from Lashley. (Cf. LASHLEY, K. S., 'Studies of Cerebral Function in Learning,' VI, *Psychol. Rev.*, 1924, 31, p. 369.)

36. TILNEY, F., AND CASAMAJOR, L., 'Myelinogeny as Applied to the Study of Behavior,' *Arch. Neur. & Psychiat.*, 1924, 12, pp. 1-66. This paper is an experimental study which aims to connect the possibility of behavior with the sheathing of the neurons. This 'myelinogenetic law' was at one time a favorite resort of the nativistic psychologists (cf. the long series of papers by Flechsig, references given by Tilney and Casamajor, *loc. cit.*). Hall made use of it. (Cf. HALL, G. S., *Adolescence*, 1904, I, p. 109.) On the basis of Watson's experimental work (*Animal Education*, 1903, pp. 1-122) it was generally abandoned. Indeed, Thorndike has said of the law that it seems 'gratuitous and improbable' (*Educational Psychology*, 1913, I, p. 229). To the present writer there seems little in the new work cited above to belie the assertion of Thorndike.

6

Imprinting

Konrad Z. Lorenz

This article originally appeared in *The Auk*, 1937, Vol. 54, pp. 245-273 (excerpted). It was chosen to illustrate the kind of observations Lorenz uses, the nature of the inductive process by which he arrives at his conclusions, and the persuasive literary style with which he presents his views.

It is a fact most surprising to the layman as well as to the zoologist that most birds do not recognize their own species 'instinctively,' but that far the greater part of their reactions, whose normal object is represented by a fellow-member of the species, must be conditioned to this object during the individual life of every bird. If we raise a young bird in strict isolation from its kind, we find very often that some or all of its social reactions can be released by other than their normal object. Young birds of most species, when reared in isolation, react to their human keeper in exactly the same way, in which under natural conditions they would respond to fellow-members of their species. In itself this phenomenon is in no way surprising. We know of a great many reflex actions that can be conditioned to very different releasing factors without being changed as to their coordination of movement. Also we know that a great many animals, when deprived of the normal object of some instinctive reaction, will respond to a substitute object, or, to be more precise, will react to other than the usual set of stimuli. In all these cases the animal will prefer the normal object as soon as it is proffered, but the bird raised in isolation refuses to react to its kind. In most cases experimentally investigated, the biologically right object, that is, the fellow-member of the species, was not even accepted as a substitute for the abnormal object, acquired under the conditions of experiment, when the latter was withdrawn and the bird left severely alone with other individuals of its species. Heinroth failed to breed hand-reared Great Horned Owls, Ravens and other birds, for no other reason than that these tame individuals responded sexually to their keepers instead of to each other. In a very few cases known, the bird whose sexual reactions were thus directed toward man, finally accepted a fellow-member of the species which, however, was always regarded as a rather poor substitute for the beloved human and was instantly abandoned whenever the latter appeared. Portielje, of the Amsterdam Zoological Gardens, raised a male of the South American Bittern (Tigrisoma) who, when mature, courted human beings. When a female was procured, he first refused to have anything to do with her but accepted her later when left alone with her for a considerable time. The birds then successfully reared a number of broods, but even then Portielje had to refrain from visiting the birds too often, because the male would, on the appearance of the former foster-father, instantly rush at the female, drive her roughly away from the nest and, turning to his keeper, perform the ceremony of nest-relief, inviting Portielje to step into the nest and incubate! What is very remarkable in all this is that while all the bird's instinctive reactions pertaining to reproduction had been repeatedly and successfully performed with the female and not once had been consummated with a human being for their object, they yet stayed irreversibly conditioned to the latter in preference to the biologically proper object. The performance or better the successful consummation of an instinctive reaction is evidently quite irrelevant for this peculiar way of acquiring its object. The object-acquiring process can be completed months before the action is executed for the first time. I once had a pair of Greylag Geese hatch a Muscovy Duck's eggs. The parent-child relations in this artificial family dissolved sooner than is normal for any of the two species, owing to some hitches in mutual understanding which occurred because the key and lock of the releasers and innate perceptory patterns of both species did not fit. From the seventh week of their life, however, the young Muscovies had nothing more to do with their former foster-parents nor with any other Greylag Geese, but behaved socially toward one another, as well as toward other members of their species as a perfectly normal Muscovy Duck should do. Ten months later the one male bird among these young Muscovies began to display sexual reactions and, to our surprise, pursued Greylag Geese instead of Muscovy Ducks, striving to copulate with them, but he made no distinction between male and female geese.

These few observational examples are sufficient to illustrate in a general way the peculiarities of the acquiring process in question, but I wish to call the reader's attention more especially to the points in which this process differs from what we call associative learning. (1) The process is confined to a very definite period of individual life, a period which in many cases is of extremely short duration; a period during which the young partridge gets its reactions of following the parent birds conditioned to their object, lasts literally but a few hours, beginning when the chick is drying off and ending before it is able to stand. (2) The process, once accomplished, is totally irreversible, so that from then on, the reaction behaves exactly like an 'unconditioned' or purely instinctive response. This absolute rigidity is something we never find in behavior acquired by associative learning, which can be unlearned or changed, at least to a certain extent. In 1936, I kept a young Greylag isolated from its kind for over a week, so that I could be sure that its following-reaction was securely attached to human beings. I then transferred this young goose to the care of a Turkey hen, whom it soon learned to use as a brooding-Kumpan for warmth instead of the electric apparatus it had hitherto favored. The gosling then followed the Turkey hen, provided that I was not in sight, and kept this up for a fortnight; but even during that time I had only to walk near the two birds, to cause the gosling to abandon the hen and follow me. I did this but three times, to avoid conditioning the gosling to my person as a leader. When, after two weeks, the gosling began to become more independent of the warming function provided by the Turkey hen, it left her and hung around our front door, waiting for a human being to emerge and trying to follow it when it did so. Now this gosling, excepting the few necessary trial runs, each of which did not last more than about a minute, had never actually consummated its following-reaction with a human for its object. On the other hand, for more than two weeks, it had been in constant contact with the Turkey hen; yet its following-reaction did not become conditioned to the Turkey in preference to the human. I would even suspect that its instinctive following-reaction was never really released by the Turkey at all, and that its following the hen was predominantly a purposive act, directed to the necessity of getting a warm-up from time to time. It never ran directly after the Turkey hen in the intensive way in which it would follow me and in which Greylag goslings follow their normal parents, but just kept near her in a most casual and deliberate sort of way, quite different from the normal reaction. Most impressive is the fact of the irreversibility of imprinting in such cases, in which birds become conditioned to an inaccessible object or to one with which it is physically impossible to perform the reaction. (3) The process of acquiring the object of a reaction is in very many cases completed long before the reaction itself has become established, as seen in the observations on the Muscovy drake cited above. This offers some difficulties to the assumption that the acquiring process in imprinting is essentially the same as in other cases of 'conditioning,' especially in associative learning. To explain the process in question as one of associative learning, one would have to assume that the reaction is, in some rudimentary stage, already present at the time when its object is irreversibly determined, an assumption which psychoanalysts would doubtless welcome, but about which I have doubts. (4) In the process of imprinting, the individual from whom the stimuli which influence the conditioning of the reaction are issuing, does not necessarily function as an object of this reaction. In many cases it is the object of the young bird's begging-reactions, or the following-reactions, in short the object of the reactions directed to the parent-companion, that irreversibly determines the conditions which, more than a year later, will release the copulating reactions in the mature bird. This is what we might call a super-individual conditioning to the species and certainly it is the chief biological task of imprinting to establish a sort of consciousness of species in the young bird, if we may use the term 'consciousness' in so broad a sense.

I would not leave the subject of imprinting without drawing the reader's attention to some very striking parallels existing between imprinting and a certain important process in the individual development of organs known in developmental mechanics (Entwicklungsmechanik) as indicative determination. If, at a certain stage of development, cellular material of a frog embryo be transplanted from one part of its body to another, the transplanted cells owing to influences emanating from their new environment, are induced to develop in a way fitting to it, and not in the way they would have developed in their original position. This process of being influenced by environment, termed 'induction' by Spemann and his school, is confined to very limited periods in the ontogenetic development of the embryo. After the lapse of this period, transplantation of tissue results in the development of abnormal monsters, because any transplanted material will develop in a way exactly fitting the place of its provenience. Also, cells transplanted before the critical time and afterward replaced in their original situation, will develop in harmony with the part of the embryo in which they are implanted during the critical period of inductive determination. It is certainly a very suggestive fact that the two chief characteristics of imprinting, in which it differs from associative learning, namely, in being irreversible and in being strictly confined to definite phases of ontogenesis, coincide with those which imprinting has in common with inductive determination in Spemann's sense of the word.

Of course, it is a matter of personal opinion how much or how little importance one should attribute to these differences from associative learning, and to analogies to inductive determination. My object in drawing the parallels to the latter, is to show that not only the phylogeny of instinctive reaction, but also its ontogeny more closely resemble those of an organ than those of any of the higher psychological processes. Also, it is a purely conceptional dispute whether imprinting is to be regarded as a special sort of learning, or as something different. The decision of this question depends entirely upon the content we see fit to assign to the conception of 'learning.' Imprinting is a process with a very limited scope, representing an acquiring process occurring only in birds and determining but one object of certain social reactions. Yet rarity does not preclude systematic importance, but I should think it rather unwise to widen the conception of learning by making it include imprinting. Such an increase of its content would bring the conception of associative learning dangerously near to including inductive determination as well, and experience has shown that this kind of stretching the boundaries of a conception is apt to destroy its value. This is exactly what has already happened to the conception of the reflex and to that of instinctive action. Since it determines the conditions for the releasing of a certain reaction, imprinting certainly must be regarded as 'conditioning' in a very broad sense of the word, but I think that English-speaking scientists should be glad to possess this term because it describes a conception less specific than that of learning.

INTERACTION BETWEEN INNATE PERCEPTORY PATTERNS AND IMPRINTING

There is a dual connection between innate perceptory patterns and the process of imprinting. On one side it is the normal function of innate perceptory patterns to guide a reaction to their biologically proper object, and we have already mentioned that sets of stimuli releasing one reaction are, strange as it may seem, factors inducing the choice-of-object of an entirely different action. For instance the sets of stimuli which, through innate perceptory patterns, release the following-mother reaction in many species of precocial birds, in doing so determine the object of sexual reactions not displayed until a year later. On the other hand, such characters of the object which are not present in the innate perceptory patterns, but to which the reactions must become conditioned in individual life, serve as a uniting factor to the different reactions once their acquisition is accomplished. This uniting of hitherto independent functions has already been illustrated by the example of the mother Mallard learning to know her ducklings individually. A very similar uniting function must be attributed to the process of imprinting as well, though it never concentrates reactions on one individual object, but only in the species as such. If normal imprinting is prevented experimentally, the social functions of a bird may be distributed between a considerable number of species. Thus, I had a tame Jackdaw, all of whose social reactions were, once for all, directed toward Hooded Crows as a species, while it could court human beings and respond with all its caring-for-progeny reactions to a young Jackdaw. One might say metaphorically, that imprinting fills out the spaces left vacant in the picture of the proper species, outlined in the bird's perceptory world by the data given by innate receptory patterns, very much as medieval artists in drawing astronomic maps, accommodated the pictures of the heraldic creatures of the zodiac between the predetermined points given by the position of the stars. Just as the imagination of such an artist is given the more freedom the smaller the number of stars which must be accommodated in the picture, so also is the scope of imprinting the greater, the fewer and the less specific are the characters of the species represented in innate perceptory patterns. With very many species it is practically impossible to direct experimentally the social reactions of the young to any but the normal object, because their innate perceptory patterns are so highly differentiated as to prevent the successful 'faking' of the corresponding sets of stimuli. This is the case with most birds of the Limicolae. Especially Curlews (Numenius arcuatus), even when hatched artificially and never having seen any living creature but their keeper, cannot be brought to respond to him with any reactions but those of escape. Most instructive are those cases where it is just possible to imitate releasing stimuli normally emanating from the parent bird, and thus to direct the imprinting of some reaction to a substitute object. This is the case with the following-mother reaction of young Mallards. It was long regarded by me as an established fact that Mallard ducklings would not accept their human keeper as a foster-parent, as would young Greylags, cranes and a number of other birds. I began experimenting by having Mallards hatched by a Muscovy Duck, with the result that they ran away from her as soon as they could, while she continued incubating on the empty shells. Foster-mother and young failed completely to respond to each other. Heinroth had exactly the same experience when he tried to let young Wood Ducks hatch under a Mallard. On the other hand I knew, from former experience, that young Mallards without any difficulty accept a spotted or even a white domestic duck as a foster-mother. The optical stimulation emanating from such a domestic duck was indeed more different from that provided by the small, brown mother Mallard, than was that of the small and rather shabby Muscovy with whom I had been experimenting. The characters relevant for the responding of innate perceptory patterns of the young must then, I concluded, be those common to the Mallard and the domestic ducks. These characters evidently were represented chiefly by the call note and by the general demeanor, both of which have not been changed much in the process of domesticating the Mallard. I decided to try experimenting on the call note which it is happily well within the powers of the human voice to imitate. I took seven young Mallards and while they were drying under the electric heater I quacked to them my imitation of the mother Mallard's call. As soon as they were able to walk, the ducklings followed me quite as closely and with quite the same reactional intensity that they would have displayed toward their real mother. I regard it as a confirmation of my preconceived opinion about the relevance of the call note, that I could not cease from quacking for any considerable period without promptly eliciting the 'lost peeping' note in the ducklings, the response given by all young anatides on having lost their mother. It was only very much later, probably after much conditioning to other characters inherent to my person, that they regarded me as their mother-companion even when I was silent.

The distribution of function between the innate perceptory patterns and the acquisition by imprinting is very different in different species. We find all possible gradations between birds like the Curlew whose innate perceptory patterns, corresponding to stimuli emanating from their own species, are so specialized as to leave hardly any room for the acquiring of characters by imprinting, up to birds like the Mallard, in which just one character, but a very 'characteristic' one, represents the evolutionarily predetermined condition which must be fulfilled to make the object 'fit' into the general pattern of the companion. Finally we know of species whose innate perceptory patterns are so reduced as to form but a very rough and sketchy outline of the companion which, under the conditions of an experiment, may become filled out by a very different object. A good example of this is represented by the reactions of the newly hatched Greylag Goose who, on coming to the light of day for the first time, looks upward in a marked manner and will respond to actually any sound or movement by giving its specific greeting reaction. If the moving and sound-emitting object begins to move away from it, the gosling will instantly start in pursuit and will most stubbornly try to follow. It has been credibly reported that boats were followed by Greylag goslings when the parent birds had been driven away, very probably at exactly the right moment to elicit the looking-up reaction above described. I intend to experiment on the general form and on the limits of size which the object, thus releasing the young gosling's following-reaction, must possess. The lack of specificity which is so remarkable in the gosling's first responses to form and sound is, to an extent, compensated by its specificity in time. The looking-up reaction once performed, it is extremely difficult and possible only by very forceful means to induce the gosling to follow any other object than the one releasing its very first greeting reaction. In a natural environment it is extremely unlikely that a moving and sound-emitting object other than the parent bird ever encounters the gosling just at the critical moment and, even if some enemy of the species should do so, it does not matter whether the still very helpless gosling runs away from it or toward it.

Another example of a species with wide and little specific innate perceptory patterns is the Shell Parakeet (Melopsittacus undulatus). I raised in isolation a young bird of this species, which was taken out of the nest of its parents at the age of about one week. It was reared in such a way as to expose it to as little stimulation from the keeper's side as possible. When fledged, it was confined to a cage in which a celluloid ball was so attached that it would swing to and fro for a considerable time if accidentally touched by the bird. My intention to transfer the sexual and general social reactions of this bird to the very simple contrivance mentioned, succeeded beyond all expectations. Very soon the bird kept continuously near the celluloid ball, edged close up to it before settling down to rest and began performing the actions of social preening with the ball for an object. Notwithstanding the fact that the celluloid ball had no feathers, the bird minutely went through all the movements of preening the short plumage of another bird's head. One most interesting item in the behavior of this bird was that evidently he was treating the celluloid ball as the head of a fellow-member of the species. All actions which he performed in connection with it were such as are normally directed toward the head of another parakeet. If the ball was attached to the bars of the cage in such a manner that the bird was at liberty to take any position relative to it by holding on to the bars, he would always do so at such a level that his own head would be at exactly the same height as the celluloid ball. When I attached it closely to a horizontal perch, so that it was much lower than the head of the sitting bird, he would be at a loss what to do with his companion and looked 'embarrassed.' Throwing the ball loosely on the floor of the cage elicited the same response as the death of the only cage-mate does in Shell Parakeets, namely, the bird fell absolutely silent and sat still in the 'fright-attitude' with feathers depressed close to the elongated body. The only instinctive reaction not normally addressed to the head of a fellow-member of the species that I could observe in this isolated bird, was the following: males in courting a female excitedly run up and down a perch in a quick sidewise movement and finally sidling up to her, they grip in a playful way at her lower back or at the base of her tail, using one foot and standing on the other. When my parakeet grew to mature age and began more seriously to court the celluloid ball, he would execute exactly the same movements, but, as he was aiming them in such a way that the ball represented the female's head, his thrust-out claw would grip only vacancy below the celluloid sphere dangling from the ceiling of his cage. All this seems to indicate that some of the innate perceptory patterns of the Shell Parakeet must, in some way, be adapted to the *receiving of formed stimuli* representing, at least in rough outline, the head and body of a companion. Portielje got analogous results in his most interesting investigation of the European Bittern (Botaurus stellaris). This bird possesses an innate perceptory pattern corresponding to formed stimuli emanating from the enemy who releases its defence-reaction. This pattern also represents the head and body and also consists of a very rough outline only. The Bittern in defending itself, strikes at the head of the enemy, not at its eyes as was formerly believed. Portielje could show that the bird in this reaction was guided by the fact that a smaller shape representing the head of the enemy, was situated just above a larger one, representing the body. Two disks of cardboard were sufficient to meet the requirements of this simple innate perceptory pattern.

The observations of the Budgerigar* may serve us as

---

* The Shell Parakeet, a corruption of Betcherrygah, native Australian for 'good parrot,' probably introduced into Great Britain at the time of the Crystal Palace Exhibition in Hyde Park, London, in 1851, when it soon became a favorite cage bird.

an example, of how, under the abnormal conditions of captivity, the rough sketch representing the companion, outlined in the bird's perceptory world by innate patterns, may be 'filled out' in an incomplete way by accepting an object only partially corresponding to the innate sketch, so that some parts of the latter are left vacant, as the space reserved for the companion's body was left vacant by the celluloid ball. Instinctive reactions directed to such vacant spaces, as the one of gripping the female's tail in the Shell Parakeet, very often prove their fundamental independence by attaching themselves to an independent object, to a separate 'Kumpan.' The Jackdaw mentioned above supplies a good example of this. More transparent perhaps and susceptible of a simpler explanation is the behavior of man-reared young Greylag Geese. This species, as mentioned before, has particularly wide and sketchy innate perceptory inlets which, by reason of their very wideness enable the experimenting human to step in and supply all the needs a Greylag has for companionship, much more completely than is possible with any other species of bird hitherto investigated. There is, however, one reaction of the Greylag which constitutes an interesting exception to this rule by having a very definite and highly differentiated 'lock,' an innate perceptory pattern corresponding to the one and only structural releaser ever evolved by the species. I am referring to the reaction of flying after another member of the flock which is dependent upon a striking and beautiful grey-and-black color pattern on the wings of the preceding bird. This color pattern which represents one of the prettiest examples of an 'automatic releaser' is quite invisible in the sitting bird, as all the parts of the wings then open to view are colored in the same 'protective' gray-brown as the rest of the bird. It is only the plumage of the propatagial membrane, which disappears beneath the shoulder plumage when the wing is folded, and furthermore the base of the remiges of the hand and their primary coverts, then covered by the dull plumage of the arm, which display a light silvery gray appearing almost white when seen at a distance. The sudden transformation of a grayish-brown bird into one predominantly black and white at the moment of taking to wing, is very impressive, even for the human observer, and most probably is essential for the following- or flocking-together reaction of the fellow-member of the species. This highly differentiated way of releasing the reaction makes it impossible for the human companion to elicit it in the isolated goose, which results in an apparently inconsistent behavior on the part of such a bird. The young goose seems to undergo a complete mental transformation at the moment of taking to wing. While being completely indifferent to any fellow-member of the species and most intensely and affectionately attached to its keeper as long as it stays on the ground or on the water, it will suddenly and surprisingly cease to respond to the human in any way whatever at the moment it takes to wing in pursuit of another Greylag. My Greylags used to follow me on my swimming tours in the Danube as a dog would, and in walking and swimming, the leader-companion of a Greylag Goose releases its following-reaction without the use of specially differentiated bodily characters; therefore, when walking or swimming in front of the bird, it is able to supply the necessary stimulation, but leaves unfulfilled the conditions releasing the following-reaction of the bird on the wing, and leaves vacant a place which may be taken by any object which supplies specific stimulation.

The releasing of one separate social reaction independently of all others which normally cooperate with it in the social life of the species, as exemplified in these observations, is indeed a very common occurrence in birds reared by man. Abnormal though these phenomena undoubtedly are, they yet tend to throw some light on the normal processes upon which social life is built up in birds. As in the case of the reflex processes, our knowledge of what is the normal sequence of reactions is almost entirely founded on a careful analysis of abnormal reactions produced experimentally.

7

Experimental Analysis of Behavior

KARL S. LASHLEY

Originally presented as a Presidential Address before the New York meeting of the American Psychological Association on April 2, 1938; also reprinted in the *Psychology Review*, 1938, Vol. 45, pp. 445-471 (excerpted).

INTRODUCTION

Some of the most remarkable observations in the literature of comparative psychology are reported in Kepner's study of Microstoma [1]. This creature related to the more familiar planaria and liver flukes, is equipped with nematocysts or stinging cells like those of the hydroids, which it discharges in defense and in capture of prey. In discharging, the stinging cell evaginates a threadlike barbed tube through which a poison is ejected. The striking fact about the creature is that it does not grow its own weapons, but captures them from another microscopic animal, the fresh water polyp, Hydra. The Hydras are eaten and digested until their undischarged stinging cells lie free in the stomach of Microstoma. The nettles are then picked up by ameboid processes of the cells lining the stomach and passed through the wall into the mesoderm. Here they are again picked up by wandering tissue cells and carried to the skin. The stinging cells are elliptical sacks with elastic walls, which are turned in at one end as a long coiled tube. In discharging, the wall of the sack contracts and forces out the barbed poison tube, from one end of the sack. The nettle cell can therefore only fire in one direction. When the mesodermal cell carries the nettle to the surface, it turns around so as to aim the poison tube outward. It then grows a trigger, and sets the apparatus to fire on appropriate stimulation.

When Microstoma has no stinging cells it captures and eats Hydras voraciously. When it gets a small supply of cells they are distributed uniformly over the surface of the body. As more cells are obtained they are interpolated at uniform intervals between those already present. When a certain concentration of cells is reached, the worm loses its appetite for Hydras and, in fact, will starve to death rather than eat any more of the polyps, which are apparently not a food but only a source of weapons.

Here, in the length of half a millimeter, are encompassed all of the major problems of dynamic psychology. There is a specific drive or appetite, satisfied only by a very indirect series of activities, with the satisfaction of the appetite dependent upon the concentration of nettles in the skin.

There are recognition and selection of a specific object, through the sensory-motor activities of the animal. Later there is recognition of the undischarged stinging cell by the wandering tissue cells, and some sort of perception of its form, so that it may be aimed. The uniform distribution of the nematocysts over the surface of the body is a splendid illustration of a Gestalt, food for speculation concerning vectors and dynamic tensions.

Actually the phenomena of growth so closely parallel those of behavior, or rather behavior parallels growth, that it is impossible to draw a sharp line between them, and animistic theories of growth have been as numerous as mechanistic theories of behavior. Kepner, in fact, postulates a group mind among the cells of the body to account for the internal behavior of Microstoma, to me a *reductio ad absurdum* of mentalistic hypotheses, whether applied to worms or man.

Nevertheless, the naturalistic literature contains many such descriptions, made by careful and accurate observers, of instinctive behavior so complex and precise in its execution that we can only stand aghast at the inadequacy of our concepts of its mechanism. Its genuine relevance to the problems of psychology is well illustrated by the classical definition of instinct as the faculty which animals have instead of intellect which yet makes their behavior seem intelligent.

I am well aware that instincts were banished from psychology some years ago, but that purge seems to have failed of its chief objective. The anti-instinct movement was aimed primarily at the postulation of imaginary forces as explanations of behavior. It was only incidental that these had also been assumed to be constitutional. The psychology of instincts was a dynamics of imaginary forces and the anti-instinct movement was primarily a crusade against such a conceptual dynamism. Somehow the argument got twisted. Heredity was made the scapegoat and the hypostatization of psychic energies goes merrily on. Desires and aversions, field forces and dynamic tensions, needs and vectors, libidoes and means-end-readinesses have the same conceptual status as had the rejected instincts and, besides, lack the one tie to physiological reality which the problem of genetic transmission gave to the latter. The anti-instinct movement was a critique of logical method which failed of effect because it was aimed at a single group of concepts. Its history is a striking example of the lack of transfer of training or the futility of formal discipline.

Although the distinction of genetic and environmental influences has little importance in many fields of psychology, it is of real significance for problems of the physiological basis of behavior. This is true because information concerning the mechanics of development and the histological organization produced by growth is far more exact than any available data concerning the changes produced by learning. Fundamental principles of neural integration may be inferred from innate structure and the behavior dependent upon it. The plasticity and variability of learned behavior precludes any similar correlations with structural patterns.

In spite of a vast literature, there have been few systematic attempts to carry the study of instincts beyond the descriptive stage. Physiologists have been preoccupied with the mechanism of the spinal reflex and students of behavior either have been content to consider instincts as constellations of reflexes clustering around external stimuli or have neglected this side of the problem entirely and, like von Bechterew [2], considered instinct as synonymous with motivation. There are actually two problems here, whose mutual relations are by no means solved. On the one hand are the more or less precise reactions to definite objects. The primiparous female rat gathers paper or other material and constructs a crude nest, cleans her young of the fetal membranes, retrieves the young to a definite locality, distinguishing them often from quite similar objects, assumes a nursing posture, and the like. These are reactions to specific stimuli. The problems which they suggest are those of neural integration; the nature of the stimulus which elicits the response, the pattern of motor activities by which a given result is achieved and, ultimately, the neuro-physiology of the behavior.

In contrast to these precise sensorimotor adjustments is the activity which can only be described as reaction to a deficit. The restless running about of the mother rat deprived of her litter, the homing of the pigeon, or the inhibition of feeding responses in the chick removed from companions presents an entirely different system of reactions from those exhibited in the presence of litter, nest or companions. This reaction to deprivation of some stimulus presents the typical problem of motivation.

For brevity I shall speak of the specific sensorimotor reactions, such as the spider's construction of a web or the courtship display of birds as the instinctive pattern, in contrast to the deficit reactions. The distinction is not always clear. When the humming-bird builds a nest she reacts specifically to lichens and fibrous material but the building to a definite form also suggests reaction to a deficit. The distinction is not a classification of activities but a suggestion of two different problems, reaction to an obvious stimulus and reaction in a situation where there is no external stimulus, or at least none as yet discovered, which is adequate to account for the observed behavior.

In many instinctive activities a further problem arises

from the periodic appearance of both the mechanism and the deficit reaction. The migration of fishes, the seasonal nesting of birds, the receptivity of the female rat during oestrus, all such periodic variations in responsiveness raise the problem of the causes of variation in the excitability of the sensorimotor mechanism and of the reaction to deficit. I shall designate this as the problem of activation of the instinct.

For a number of years we have been trying to discover the mechanism underlying the reproductive behavior of animals. This activity was chosen for study because it presents the most precise instinctive behavior of mammals which can be brought under laboratory observation and because it exhibits a wide variety of problems, both of integrated behavior and of motivation. The work has developed in several directions. I shall summarize the results and attempt to relate them to some of the more general problems of the mechanism of behavior.

THE DISTINCTION OF REFLEX AND INSTINCT

The changes in the character of the responses and in the nature of the adequate stimulus under different environmental conditions, for example the cleaning of the young in the nest and not during retrieving and the like, are, in a sense, a confirmation of the chain-reflex theory of instinct. It is true that the instinctive behavior creates situations which in turn serve as stimuli to further activities. To dismiss the activity as reflex is, however, to ignore its characteristic features.

Many writers have attempted to differentiate between reflex and instinct, but the final criterion has been only a vague difference in complexity. Our conception of the nature of reflex is derived largely from avoiding reactions elicited by protopathic stimuli and from the muscle-shortening reflexes. These are elicited by a localized group of sensory endings. Locus, intensity and modality of the stimulus are its determining properties. In contrast to this, sexual and maternal behavior seem chiefly determined by the pattern of organization of the stimulus, with locus of incidence upon the sensory surface or sense modality secondary. In this respect the instincts present the organismal problem as the reflexes do not. This difference in the nature of the adequate stimulus justifies, I believe, the retention of the term instinct to stress the importance of the problem of sensory organization.

THE ACTIVATION OF THE SENSORIMOTOR SYSTEM

Many sensorimotor reactions are performed apparently as soon as the growth of essential nervous structures is completed. The pioneer studies of Herrick and Coghill [3] marked the way for the many later investigations correlating the appearance of early reflexes with the growth of nervous connections. In many of the early reflexes the mechanism is capable of functioning as soon as growth is completed. But there are, also, many activities which appear only at some interval after the completion of neuron growth. The work of Tilney and Casamajor [4] suggests that the late appearance of some of the so-called delayed reflexes or instincts may be due to late myelinization of tracts, but the maturation of instinct as studied by Breed [5] and Bird [6] is probably due to a diversity of causes in which neural growth is less important than general development of muscular strength and control.

Reproductive behavior presents a unique situation among instinctive activities in that it is delayed long after the development of the nervous system and is conditioned by the attainment of sexual maturity. Recent studies of hormonal activation of sexual behavior raise important problems, both of neural integration and of motivation. The work of Steinach [7], Stone [8] and a number of more recent investigators shows the dependence of the behavior of the male upon the testicular hormone. Many studies show the importance of endocrine products in the regulation of the oestrus cycle and the relation of the behavior of the female to this cycle. The experiments of Wiesner and Sheard [9], Riddle [10, 11], and others indicate something of the dependence of maternal behavior upon pituitary secretions.

The interrelations of the hormones are complex and

the literature upon this subject is vast. I shall not take time to review the evidence on the physiological action of the various hormones. More important for us who are interested in behavior than the details of the biochemistry and interaction of the endocrine products is the question of how they act to induce the appearance of specific patterns of behavior. The introduction of male hormone into the blood stream somehow sensitizes the animal to the stimuli presented by the female in heat. What is the mechanism of such sensitization?

The difficulty of the problem is enormously increased by the variability of behavior under normal conditions. There seems to be no item of behavior except parturition and the removal of the fetal membranes from the young which is wholly restricted to the mother rat. Norman has found that nests are sometimes built and young retrieved in a manner indistinguishable from that of the best mothers by virgin females and even by males. Stone and others have observed female mating reactions on the part of normal males and Beach the masculine behavior of normal virgin females. The mere observation of such behavior in experiments involving injections of a hormone therefore does not justify the conclusion that the hormone is responsible for the behavior. There are distinguishing characteristics of what we have considered as normal behavior. The parturient female collects her young into the nest immediately or within a few hours after their birth. Virgin females and males show such behavior only after much longer exposure to young, often with an intervening period during which the young are devoured. It is not impossible to establish definite criteria by which hormonal effects may be recognized but the necessary criteria are quantitative rather than qualitative. The validity of the criteria employed by earlier workers is somewhat called in question. We can only consider the problem of activation on the basis of observations which should be checked again with more attention to the range of normal variation.

With this reservation it seems worth while to consider the mechanism of activation, if only to define the problem more clearly.

1. Does the hormone stimulate the growth or formation of new nervous connections, as the chemical organizers in Spemann's experiments stimulate differentiation of structure? A number of observations may be urged as arguments against this possibility. Castration abolishes the male reaction. Injection of the male hormone may restore it promptly and it may be repeatedly revived by repeated injection of the hormone. It is unlikely that each of these repeated activations involves a renewed growth with intervening degeneration of the mechanism. In the experiments of Wiesner and Sheard retrieving of the young grew less persistent as the young approached weaning age and began to venture from the nest. The retrieving reaction could be restored to its initial vigor, either by injection of pituitary hormones or by giving the mother new-born young to nurse. The responses to the younger infants were apparently immediate. We cannot ascribe the initiation of neuron growth to this stimulus and so have no reason to assume that the hormone produces such an effect. This and other evidence points to the conclusions that the neural mechanism is already laid down before the action of the hormone, and that the latter is only an activator, increasing the excitability of a mechanism already present.

2. Does the hormone act merely by increasing the general excitability of the organism? Reduced sexual activity during starvation or physical illness [Stone, 12] and the fact that male hormone increases the excitability of the sympathetic system as measured by vasomotor reflexes [Wheelon and Shipley, 13] lends plausibility to this assumption. I have found, however, that castration does not alter general activity for a month or so, nor is there other valid evidence for a reduction in general excitability which is common to castrated males, females in the dioestrum, and nonparturient females, which should be the case if the hormones acted as general excitants. Finally, the strongest argument against this hypothesis is the apparent specificity of the different hormones for different patterns of behavior as illustrated by Moore's reversal of sex behavior [14] by interchanging the gonads of the two sexes.

3. The hormones induce specific changes in various organs, such as the vascular changes in the uterine mucosa, the rapid enlargement of the testis, or lactation in the mammary glands. It is possible that these altered states initiate sensory impulses which facilitate the mechanisms of the secondary sexual reactions. This is the mechanism implied in Moll's evacuation theory [15] of the sex drive and in the ascription of various phases of maternal behavior to lactation. The suppression of the oestrus cycle and of receptivity in the female rat during lactation, and the correlation of sexual behavior with phases of the oestrus cycle suggest an elaborate interplay of such mechanisms.

The evidence against this somatic sensory reinforcement is rather compelling, however. Stone tested the evacuation theory by removing as much as possible of the reproductive system from males and observing their behavior after treatment with male hormone. He found sexual excitability, responsiveness to the female in heat, in castrated animals from which all of the accessory reproductive glands had been removed, leaving no anatomic basis for the tension of accumulated secretions assumed as the source of sensory reinforcement in the evacuation theory. Several investigators [Wiesner and Mirskaia, 16] have reported the hormonal induction of oestrus without the induction of mating behavior. Ball [17] has observed the normal signs of sexual excitement in females from which the uterus and vagina had been removed. Wiesner and Sheard have reported and Norman has confirmed the fact that normal retrieving of young occurs in parturient females from which the mammary glands were removed in infancy. The mechanical stimuli of lactation therefore cannot be an important factor in the induction of this phase of maternal behavior.

In each of these experiments the organs to which the function of sensory reinforcement would naturally be ascribed have been removed without abolishing excitability to the appropriate stimuli. Still more conclusive evidence on this matter comes from instances of reversal of sexual behavior. In gynandromorphic insects with head of one sex, thorax and abdomen of the other, sexual behavior is reported to follow the sex of the head, not that of the reproductive system [Whiting, 18]. Reversal of sexual behavior in hens with tumors of the ovary has long been known [Morgan, 19]. In the experiments of Moore the gonads were interchanged between male and female rats and corresponding reversal of behavior noted, the feminized males retrieving young and the masculinized females showing male behavior.

Such observations and experiments seem to preclude the evacuation theory of sexual activation and to minimize the importance of any sensory reinforcement from somatic organs in the production of specific reproductive responses. Of course, they do not rule out all possible peripheral mechanisms which might provide effective facilitation for specific reflexes. Certain possibilities have not yet been explored, such as that of an altered temperature control during pregnancy which might precipitate nest building, as Kinder [20] has suggested, or localized changes in vasomotor reflexes which might alter local cutaneous sensitivity. Nevertheless, the organs showing greatest structural changes under hormone influences and those to which sensory facilitation has been ascribed have been removed without destroying the secondary sexual reactions and the observations on reversal of sexual behavior make it pretty certain that somatic sensory impulses cannot be the determiners of specific reaction patterns.

4. There remains only the last alternative, that the hormones act upon the central nervous system to increase the excitability of the sensorimotor mechanism specifically involved in the instinctive activity. Direct evidence for this is lacking and we have no conception of the way in which various organic compounds might exercise a selective effect upon specific nervous elements of schemata. There are, however, many instances of the restricted influence of drugs, both upon localized structures, as in the case of strychnine, and upon psychological functions, as in the action of mescal. There is also some slight evidence for the local sensitization of nervous tissue to organic toxins, with a selective action of later doses upon the sensitized tissue. The hypothesis of a specific action

of the hormones upon nervous organization is therefore not without parallel in the literature of pharmacology. The problem here is clear enough. Techniques of direct investigation, as by serological tests of the affinity of specific structures for different hormones, are still lacking.

REFERENCES

1. KEPNER, W. A., *Animals Looking into the Future*, New York: Macmillan, 1925, pp. 197.
2. BECHTEREW, W. V., *La psychologie objective*, Paris: Alcan, 1913, iii plus 478.
3. HERRICK, C. J. AND COGHILL, C. E., The development of reflex mechanisms in Amblystoma, *J. Comp. Neurol.*, 1915, 25, 68-86.
4. TILNEY, F. AND CASAMAJOR, L., Myelinogeny as applied to the study of behavior, *Arch. Neurol. Psychiat.*, 1924, 12, 1-66.
5. BREED, F. S., Maturation and use in the development of instinct, *J. Animal Behav.*, 1913, 3, 274-285.
6. BIRD, C., The effect of maturation upon the pecking instinct of chicks, *Ped. Sem.*, 1926, 33, 212-233.
7. STEINACH, E., Geschlechtstrieb und echt sekundäre Geschlechtsmerkmale als Folge der innersekretorischen Funktion der Keimdrüsen, *Zentbl.f.Physiol.*, 1910, 24, 551.
8. STONE, C. P. The congenital sexual behavior of the young male albino rat, *J. Comp. Psychol.*, 1922, 2, 95-152.
9. ———, AND SHEARD, N. M., *Maternal Behavior in the Rat*, Edinburgh: Oliver, 1933, XI, 245.
10. RIDDLE, D., LAHR, E. L. AND BATES, R. W., Maternal behavior induced in virgin rats by prolactin, *Proc. Soc. Exp. Biol. Med.*, 1935, 32, 730-734.
11. ———, Aspects and implications of hormonal control of the maternal instinct, *Proc. Amer. Phil. Soc.*, 1935, 75, 521-525.
12. ———, Delay in the awakening of copulatory ability in the male albino rat incurred by defective diets. I. Quantitative deficiency, *J. Comp. Psychol.*, 1924b,

4, 195-224, II. Qualitative deficiency, *J. Comp. Psychol.*, 1925a, 5, 177-203.
13. WHEELON, H. AND SHIPLEY, J. L., The effects of testicular transplants upon vasomotor irritability, *Amer. J. Physiol.*, 1915, 39, 395-400.
14. MOORE, C. R., On the physiological properties of the gonads as controllers of somatic and psychical characteristics. I. The rat, *J. Exper. Zool.*, 1919, 28, 137.
15. MOLL, A., *Handbuch der Sexualwissenschaften*, Leipzig: F. C. W. Vogel, 1926, 2 vol.
16. WIESNER, B. P., AND MIRSKAIA, L., On the endocrine basis of mating in the mouse, *J. Exper. Physiol.*, 1939, 20, 273-279.
17. BALL, J. Sex Behavior of the rat after removal of the uterus and vagina, *J. Comp. Psychol.*, 1934, 18, 419-422.
18. WHITING, P. W., AND WENSTRUP, E. J., Fertile gynandromorphs in Habrobracon, *J. Hered.*, 1932, 23, 31-38.
19. MORGAN, T. H., *Heredity and Sex*, New York: Columbia Univ. Press, 1914, p. 284.
20. KINDER, E. F., A study of the nest-building activity of the albino rat, *J. Exper. Zool.*, 1927, 47, 117-161.

8

Introduction of Mating Behavior in Male and Female Chicks Following Injection of Sex Hormones

GLADWYN K. NOBLE AND ARTHUR ZITRIN

This article originally appeared in *Endocrinology*, 1942, Vol. 30, pp. 327-334 (excerpted).

The investigation was supported by a grant to the senior author from the Committee for Research in Problems of Sex, National Research Council. The death of the senior author occurred before experiments herein reported were completed.

This article represents, in part, material submitted by the junior author in partial fulfillment of the requirements for the degree of Master of Science, New York University.

The use of gonadotropic and gonadal hormones to produce some of the elements of adult behavior in male chicks has been reported by several earlier workers. Domm and Van Dyke [1] and Domm [2] observed that male chicks began to crow at 9 days of age following 6 daily injections of pituitary gonadotropin. Attempts at treading appeared in these birds at 13 days, after 10 daily injections. Hamilton [3] injected male chicks with 0.5 mg. of testosterone propionate daily for 27 days, starting from the second day after hatching. The birds first crowed 180 hours after the initial injection, and later showed cock-like fighting and 'wing-flapping.' However, Hamilton did not report treading or other signs of copulatory aggressiveness on the part of the injected males. Horn [4] injected testosterone propionate into young chicks and obtained behavior identical to that described by Hamilton [3]. Breneman [5] reported crowing in male chicks 5 days old after the injection of either testosterone propionate or dihydro-androsterone benzoate.

Noble and Wurm [6] induced copulation in an immature Black-crowned Night Heron following testosterone propionate injections. In the male rat, Stone [7] reported that by daily injections of testosterone propionate on and after the ages of 22 to 26 days, the median age of first copulation was set ahead of that of controls by about 20 days.

One purpose of the present investigation was to determine whether the complete copulatory pattern of the adult cock can be induced in male chicks injected with testosterone propionate. The findings of Hamilton [3], Breneman [5] and of Horn [4] do not prove that such behavior can be elicited in immature androgen-injected birds. Although pituitary gonadotropin produces attempts at treading, the complete mating pattern has never been reported. A second objective of this work was to attempt to produce sexual receptivity and the accompanying 'squatting' behavior characteristic of adult hens, in estrogen-injected female chicks.

MATERIALS AND METHODS

All of the chicks employed in this work were single-comb White Leghorns, sexed at hatching and received at our laboratory when 2 days of age. A total of 63 chicks was divided into two experimental series and studied at different dates; the birds used in *Experiment I* were taken from a different batch than those used in the later work. For all hormone injections the vehicle used was 0.1 cc. of sesame oil.

EXPERIMENT I

Group A. This group consisted of twelve 15-day-old male chicks. Six males received 27 daily intramuscular injections of 0.5 mg. of testosterone propionate.* The

---

* Testosterone propionate (Oreton) and estradiol benzoate (Progynon-B) were supplied by the Schering Corporation, Bloomfield, New Jersey.

other 6 chicks were kept as controls and received daily injections of 0.1 cc. of pure sesame oil. All injections were made into the breast muscles, the side and site of injection being varied systematically from day to day.

Group B. Twelve female chicks, 15 days old, were divided equally into experimental and control groups. Six experimental chicks received 27 daily injections of 0.17 mg. of estradiol benzoate,* while the controls received 0.1 cc. of sesame oil. The injections were carried out in a manner similar to that described for the males.

The weights of all chicks were recorded on the day of the first injection, 24 hours after the last injection, and again 37 days later.

EXPERIMENT II

Group A. Ten 2-day-old male chicks received daily injections of 0.5 mg. of testosterone propionate for 34 days. Nine chicks of the same age were employed as controls and were injected with 0.1 cc. of pure sesame oil daily.

Group B. Four 2-day-old male chicks were removed from the flock and each was raised in complete isolation. The isolated birds received daily injections of 0.5 mg. of testosterone propionate for 34 days.

Group C. Ten 2-day-old females received 31 daily injections of 0.17 mg. of estradiol benzoate, over a period of 34 days. Five other females of the same age were given the same number of injections of 0.08 mg. of estradiol benzoate. Eleven control pullets were injected with pure sesame oil. No injections were given to the experimental and control chicks in this group on the 20th, 22nd, and 24th day of the experiment.

For the first week all the chicks in Experiment II received subcutaneous injections of the hormones. Starting on the 8th day all injections were given intramuscularly, in order to reduce the possibility of leakage from the site

* Testosterone propionate (Oreton) and estradiol benzoate (Progynon-B) were supplied by the Schering Corporation, Bloomfield, New Jersey.

of injection. The weights of all of the birds in this experiment were recorded weekly, as were the comb sizes of all of the males. The weights and comb sizes of all males were taken again 3 weeks after the last injection. Throughout this work an effort was made to maintain, as far as was possible, similar conditions of food supply, heat, light, crowding, and hygiene, for experimental and control birds.

METHODS OF OBSERVATION AND TESTING

Experiment I. Observations for behavior were made daily for about 2½ hours. During this period all the birds were kept in a large runway, lighted from the inside and constructed so that they would not be subjected to outside disturbances. After the first attempts at treading were seen each male was tested in an individual cage with a deeply anesthetized chick, and observations of sexual behavior were recorded. A dead chick was found to suit the purpose just as well, and was later substituted for the anesthetized bird. On the 16th day of the experiment each experimental male was paired with an injected female and placed in an individual cage. The cages were arranged so that the occupants of all could be seen at one time. The male-female pairs were then observed for about 2½ hours daily, and copulation and other sexual behavior were recorded. Frequent substitutions of control females for injected ones were made so that all of the pullets were under observation while paired with males.

Experiment II. The same general plan employed in Experiment I was used in observing and testing the chicks of this series. The isolated birds were observed for crowing behavior for a maximum of 1 hour daily and were later tested for treading after all the injected males of group A had exhibited this reaction. Both control and experimental females of group C were paired with the injected males at some time during the course of the experiment. The pairs in this experiment were observed for a minimum of 4 hours daily.

NORMAL MATING BEHAVIOR

Copulation in the domestic fowl is generally preceded by a brief courtship in which the male unfolds one wing and skips with little mincing steps in an arc around the female. Skard [8] refers to this behavior as "dancing," while Murchison [9] calls it the "sex invitation." It is the latter term which we shall use. A description of the male's copulatory behavior is given by Skard [8].

The overt sexual behavior of the female is much more passive than that of the cock, and as a result is more difficult to describe. Sometimes the hen will squat spontaneously at the approach of a male, or in answer to his sex invitation. This squatting can be distinguished from the normal crouching of the bird by the fact that in the former case the front part of the body is held lower than the back part, and the tail is raised. Squatting in reply to the cock's clear-cut sexual aggressiveness is the more general case, however. When the male seizes the neck feathers of the female or mounts with one or both feet, the hen may crouch submissively and raise her tail feathers up and to one side so that the contact of the ani can be made. Sometimes the male forces the female down before she submits. It is significant that the number of the male's copulatory attempts always exceeds the number of consummated copulations [8].

As far as we have been able to determine, attempts at copulation do not normally appear until about 4½ months of age. Hens will not submit to copulation until a little later than this, occasionally not until after the first egg-laying.

EXPERIMENTAL RESULTS

Experiment I

Behavior of Males. All injected males were first observed to crow on the 4th day, following 3 daily injections of testosterone propionate. At this time crowing occurred infrequently and was of extremely short duration. Hamilton [3] gives an excellent description of the juvenile crow of the chicks, as well as the posture which accompanies it. After 6 injections the chicks exhibited the vicious cocklike fighting and frequent 'wing-flapping' also mentioned by Hamilton. Control males seldom pecked at each other and showed no fighting or crowing.

On the 8th day of the experiment 2 injected birds displayed behavior resembling weak attempts at treading. On the following day, after 8 injections, all of the experimental males exhibited this reaction. Raising of the male's neck feathers when approaching a female, and pecking at her head characterized this activity. Some of the males were also seen attempting to mount a sleeping or crouching female, but such attempts were never vigorously prosecuted.

After 9 injections 4 of the 6 experimental males showed the adult copulatory pattern in treading an anesthetized chick. Except for the absence of the sex invitation and the actual anal contact, this behavior did not differ from that of the mature cock. By the following day all 6 injected birds treaded an anesthetized chick. In most cases the response to the prostrate bird was almost immediate, and numerous treadings of this kind were recorded. Occasionally, it was observed, some of the chicks mounted obliquely or gripped the tail or wing feathers and executed all the copulatory movements although not correctly mounted on the reclining bird. This behavior, however, was uncommon and generally not exhibited in later tests. Attempts to mount live birds were always oriented in the normal fashion. The sex invitation was first observed on the 11th day; it was directed toward a dead chick. Throughout the experiment this preliminary courtship was seen only rarely. After the injected males had been paired with females for several days, the copulatory response to a dead or anesthetized bird was not elicited as frequently or as quickly as was the case in earlier tests.

In addition to treading, another indication of the cock-like behavior of the injected male chicks was revealed by a type of activity less obviously sexual. The males very often called the females to food before eating, or scratched the ground to find food and then held it in their beaks while calling to the female, simulating in this way the behavior of the adult.

Behavior of Females. The first normal squatting behavior by an injected female was observed on the 16th experimental day, following 17 injections of estradiol benzoate. By the 26th day all of the experimental females had been seen to squat for a treading male at least once. At the conclusion of the experiment a total of 31 treadings had been observed in which both the male and female exhibited typically adult behavior. Individual differences were apparent. One female was observed to squat 17 times, whereas in another this behavior was seen only once. The other 4 injected females exhibited the squatting reaction, 2, 2, 3, and 6 times during the period of observation. Two of the 6 birds were particularly passive and were seen to squat as soon as the males with which they were paired attempted copulation. None of the control females permitted treading when paired with the injected males.

Experiment II

Behavior of Males. Seven of the injected chicks crowed less than 40 hours after receiving the first injection, when they were not yet 4 days old. They had received 1 mg. of testosterone propionate. On the following day all injected males except one of the isolated birds were heard crowing. This latter bird was first seen to crow on the 9th day of the experiment. Since the isolated chicks were under observation for only 1 hour each day it is possible that this bird crowed when no observer was present.

Treading of a dead chick first occurred on the 13th day of the experiment. As in Experiment I this behavior was characterized by the execution of all the movements exhibited by the adult cock during copulation. After pairing with females the males showed persistent copulatory attempts but the pullets were never observed to squat. Very often a male would mount a struggling female and execute all the copulatory movements while being carried around the cage on her back. While no extensive records of attempts at copulation were kept, the following figures will give some idea of the strength of the male's tendency to mate. In 2 hours of observation one male made 23 attempts at treading. In 6 cases the male had seized the neck feathers of the female and had mounted with both feet, only to be thrown from her back as she fled. As was the case with the males in Experiment I the sex invitation was rarely exhibited by these chicks.

The birds raised in isolation not only crowed and treaded as early as the males of group A, but also showed other behavior peculiar to themselves. After less than 2 weeks of isolation it was observed that when the experimenter's hand was put into the cage of one of these birds, the chick would peck at it viciously and very often fight it as if he were fighting with another chick. This activity was in marked contrast to the behavior of the birds raised together who fled at the approach of the hand. On the 24th day of the experiment one of the isolated males extended the sex invitation to the hand of the observer, then mounted, gripped the skin tightly and went through all the movements of the copulatory act. The other isolated birds subsequently showed this behavior, its appearance being easily elicited when the observer put his hand into their cages.

Behavior of Females. The injected pullets of this experiment did not exhibit the adult sexual behavior which was expected because of the findings in the earlier study. Although they were under observation for much longer periods of time each day than were the birds in Experiment I, none of the chicks was ever seen to squat for a treading male. No difference in behavior between the injected and control females could be discerned. The numerous treading attempts of the injected males, and the partially denuded necks of the females where they had been seized, gave ample evidence of the male's sex drive, but no indication of female sexual behavior was ever observed.

Comb Growth. Within a few days after the first injection of testosterone propionate there was a noticeable

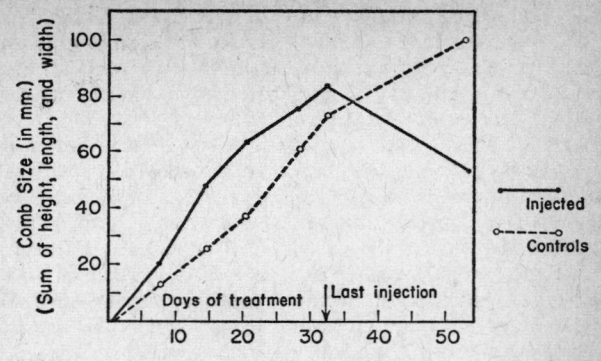

Fig. 1. Comb growth in control and androgen-injected chicks.

growth of the experimental males' combs. They soon became large, turgid, and extremely thick throughout, and in about 2 weeks had assumed a deep red hue. There was a comparable growth of the wattles, and the earlobes also were larger and more deeply colored than those of the controls. When injections were stopped there was a rapid regression of the combs, so that 3 weeks after the last injection the combs of the controls were considerably larger than those of the experimental chicks. Figure 1 illustrates the comb growth of all male chicks during the course of this experiment.

There was no discernible difference in size between the combs of injected females and those of the controls.

DISCUSSION

Behavior

Males. The psycho-sexual changes accompanying puberty represent the maturation of some of the most complex of the group of delayed instincts. Mating, for example, is an activity that generally requires the execution of complicated, coordinated movements by the male, and which appears, in lower vertebrates at least, fully integrated at maturity without previous practice or learning. That mating behavior in the male fowl is dependent upon the active secretion of testicular hormone is indicated by experiments on castration, implantation, and injection. Reviews of the literature on these subjects can be found in references 10 and 11.

In our experiments the behavior pattern involved in copulation by the adult cock was induced in its entirety in immature male chicks after the injection of testosterone propionate. This activity was manifested long before somatic maturity was reached, and antedate its normal appearance by several months. Treading a dead or anesthetized bird may be peculiar to those birds receiving heavy doses of male hormone, since testing a normal sexually-active cock in this manner did not elicit the copulatory response. It is significant, however, that after the injected males had been paired with females for a short time the dead chicks did not serve as adequate stimuli for eliciting copulatory behavior as often as they did earlier in the experiment.

The behavior of the injected males raised apart from their fellows in reacting sexually toward humans, is very similar to that described by Craig [12] for male doves which matured in isolation, and by Lorenz [13] for hand-reared Great-Horned Owls, Ravens, "and other birds."

Females. The extensive work of Domm [14] on ovariotomy in the fowl seems to prove quite conclusively that the presence of a functional ovary is essential for normal sex behavior of the hen. Birds in which the left ovary and later the right compensatory gonad were removed assumed a neutral behavior resembling that of a capon. They exhibited none of the sexual behavior of either sex and were never observed to squat for a treading male. Allee and Collias [15] report the case of such a bird which, following injections with estradiol, squatted for a cock. This poulard was known to have previously repeatedly avoided the solicitations of sexually active males.

In the light of the above work it was thought possible to produce female sex behavior in estrogen-injected pullets, just as it was possible to induce masculinization in androgen-injected immature males. Our expectations were realized in Experiment I in which chicks injected with estradiol benzoate starting on the 15th day of age had all squatted for a treading male after 18 to 26 injections. In Experiment II, however, in which injections were started on the second day after hatching, no squatting was ever observed. The difference in behavior between the females of the two experiments presents a perplexing problem for which further study may provide a solution. It is possible, of course, that squatting occurred when the birds were not under observation. We do not consider this a likely occurrence. The male-female pairs were observed for longer periods of time than were those in Experiment I, and at various hours of the day, including early morning and late evening. It is felt that if squatting occurred at all it would have been seen in at least one case.

Comb Growth

Males. Breneman [18, 19] found that after the injection of small doses of either testosterone propionate or dihydro-androsterone benzoate the chicks' combs did not retrogress, but continued to grow unabated. In the earlier work [18] he also reported that there was a temporary inhibition of testes growth which lasted through the injection period. In Experiment II we injected chicks with larger doses of testosterone propionate than were used by Breneman, and over a considerably longer period of time. Within 3 weeks after the last injection the combs had retrogressed to a point where they were exceeded in size by the control combs by a considerable amount. This would seem to indicate that when large doses of androgen are injected into chicks, an inhibition of the testes is obtained which is effective for some tiime after injections are stopped.

Females. The findings of Dorfman and Greulich [20] and Munro and Kosin [17] indicate that none of the estrogens has an effect on comb growth of female chicks. Uotila [21], however, found that estrogen-injected pullets had combs slightly smaller than controls. Juhn, Gustavson, and Gallagher [22] reported that urinary estrogens did not affect significantly the combs of older birds. Allee and Colias [15] mention similar results obtained with estradiol, but add that heavy treatment with the estrogen caused comb involution. In our work we observed no difference between the combs of experimental and control female chicks.

SUMMARY

Male chicks injected with testosterone propionate exhibited all the sexual behavior patterns of the adult cock. Crowing appeared as early as the 4th day of age and treading was seen on the 15th day. The copulatory pattern was identical to that of the sexually mature bird. Injected males raised in isolation crowed and treaded as early as other treated birds. In addition, the experimenter could serve as 'a releaser' for some of the social and sexual reactions of these chicks which normally are directed only toward other birds of the same species.

Females injected with estradiol benzoate starting on the 15th day of age squatted for treading males after 18 to 26 daily treatments. The behavior was typically that of a sexually receptive hen. Chicks in which hormone treatment was initiated on the 2nd day of age did not exhibit this behavior.

The growth rate of experimental males was uniformly depressed. Augmentation or depression of growth rate was obtained in estrogen-injected females, depending upon the age of the birds, and the dosages administered.

The combs of experimental males retrogressed after the cessation of male hormone treatment to a considerably smaller size than those of controls. Female combs were unaffected by estrogen treatment.

REFERENCES

1. DOMM, L. V., AND H. B. VAN DYKE: *Proc. Soc. Exper. Biol. & Med.* 30: 349. 1932.
2. DOMM, L. V.: *C. S. H. Symp. on Quant. Biol.* 5: 241. 1937.
3. HAMILTON, J. B.: *Endocrinology* 23: 53. 1938.
4. HORN, C. A.: *Proc. Pa. Acad. Sci.* 14: 27. 1940.
5. BRENEMAN, W. R.: *Endocrinology* 24: 55. 1939.

6. Noble, G. K., and M. Wurm: *Endocrinology* 26: 837. 1940.
7. Stone, C. P.: *Endocrinology* 26: 511. 1940.
8. Skard, A. G.: *Acta Psychologica* 2: 175. 1937.
9. Murchison, C.: *J. Genet. Psychol.* 46: 76. 1935.
10. Carpenter, C. R.: *Psych. Bull.* 29: 509. 1932.
11. Allen, E.: *Sex and Internal Secretions*, Baltimore: The Williams and Wilkins Co., 1939.
12. Craig, W.: *J. Animal Behavior* 4: 121. 1914.
13. Lorenz, K. Z.: *The Auk* 54: 245. 1937.
14. Domm, L. V.: *J. Exper. Zool.* 48: 31. 1927.
15. Allee, W. C., and N. Collias: *Endocrinology* 27: 87/ 1940.
16. Juhn, M., and R. C. Gustavson: *J. Exper. Zool.* 56: 31. 1930.
17. Munro, S. S., and I. L. Kosin: *Endocrinology* 27: 687. 1940.
18. Breneman, W. R.: *Endocrinology* 21: 503. 1937.
19. Breneman, W. R.: *Endocrinology* 23: 44. 1938.
20. Dorfman, R. I., and W. W. Greulich: *Yale J. Biol. & Med.* 10: 79. 1937.
21. Uotila, U. U.: *Anat. Rec.* 74: 165. 1939.
22. Juhn, M., R. C. Gustavson and T. F. Gallagher: *J. Exper. Zool.* 64: 133. 1932.

9

The Effects of Meprobamate on Imprinting in Waterfowl

ECKHARD H. HESS

This article originally appeared in the *Annals* of the New York Academy of Science, 1956-57, Vol. 67, pp. 724-733.

The work described in this paper was supported in part by Grant M-776 of the National Institutes of Health, Public Health Services, Department of Health, Education and Welfare, Bethesda, Md., and by the Wallace C. and Clara A. Abbott Memorial Fund of the University of Chicago, Chicago, Ill. The meprobamate (Miltown) was furnished by the Wallace Laboratories, New Brunswick, N. J.

To discuss properly the effects of meprobamate on the imprinting process it is necessary to give an account of the phenomenon of imprinting and the methods with which it is studied in our laboratory. The first section of this paper therefore will give a brief account of our general approach to the problem and the particular results that bear on the present study.

Students of behavior generally agree that the early experiences of the organism have a profound effect upon adult behavior. The literature in this field has recently been reviewed by Beach and Jaynes [1]. Hebb [2] has given us the rule that the effect of early experience upon adult behavior is inversely correlated with age. Our problem, then, is not so much to determine whether early experience is important in determining adult behavior as it is to decide how these results are accomplished.

Three somewhat different statements concerning this problem are usually made in the contemporary literature. The first of these is that early habits are very persistent and may prevent the formation of new ones. The second is that early perceptual learning profoundly affects all future learning. This theory leads to the very difficult problem of whether basic perceptions are inherited or acquired. Experimental procedures used here usually consist of preventing the subject from using some sense modality for a period of time and then comparing his behavior with controls of the same age who have had the opportunity of using that modality. Results are difficult to interpret, as this procedure often results in degenerative changes in the sense organ involved. The third of these statements is that early social contacts determine adult social behavior. This is imprinting.

At the turn of the century, Craig [3], experimenting with wild pigeons, found that in order to cross two different species it was first necessary to rear the young of one species under the adults of the other. Upon reaching maturity the birds so reared preferred mates of the same species as their foster parents. Other intersexual fixations have been observed in birds and fishes.

Heinroth [4, 5] and his wife successfully reared by hand the young of almost every species of European bird. They found that many of the social responses of these birds were transferred to their human caretaker. Lorenz [6] extended these experiments, dealing especially with grayleg geese. Lorenz also was the first to point out the fact that there are certain critical periods in the animal's life in which such modification of behavior occurs. Ramsay and Hess [7] have found the critical age for the imprinting of mallard ducklings on their parents to be at twelve to seventeen hours after hatching. In addition, Lorenz postulated that, in imprinting, the first object to release a social response becomes the only one to release at maturity not only that particular response, but other related social responses. As has been pointed out repeatedly in the literature, then, imprinting is not only related to the problem of behavior, but also to the general biological problem of evolution and speciation.

Although studied mainly in birds, [8, 9] examples of imprinting have been reported in insects [10], in fish [11], and in some mammals. Those mammals in which the phenomenon has been reported (sheep, 12, deer, 13, and buffalo, 14) are all animals in which the young are almost immediately mobile when born. Experimental work with mammals has, however, not been done within the framework presented here.

Genetic studies with two species of fowl that I began in 1955 now indicate that imprintability is inherited and can be bred into or out of a strain. Further experiments with cochin bantams indicate that the inheritance of imprintability is probably sex-linked.

Briefly then, imprinting has been represented as an extremely rapid form of learning that takes place in the early life of many organisms and that is possible only during a very brief period in the life of those organisms.

TESTING PROCEDURE

Subject. The subjects were mallard ducklings, although similar experiments were also carried out with other species of fowl.

Apparatus. The apparatus we constructed to be used in imprinting consisted of a circular runway about 5 ft. in diameter. This runway was 12 in. wide and 12½ ft. in circumference at the center. Boundaries were formed by walls of Plexiglas 12 in. high. A mallard duck decoy, suspended from an elevated arm radiating from the center of the apparatus, was fitted internally with a loudspeaker and a heating element. It was held about 2 in. above the center of the runway. The arms suspending the decoy would be rotated by either one of 2 variable-speed motors. The speed of rotation and intermittent movement could be regulated from the control panel located about 5 feet from the apparatus. The number of rotations of both the decoy and the animal were recorded automatically. Tape recorders with continuous tapes provided the sound that was played through the speaker of the decoy. A trap door in the runway, actuated from the control panel, would return the duckling to its box.

Preliminary Procedure. Mallard eggs were collected from nest boxes located in a duck-pond area. After storage for a few days, they were incubated in a dark forced-air incubator. About 2 days before hatching, the eggs were transferred to a hatching incubator. Precautions were taken to place each newly hatched bird into a small cardboard box (5 x 4 x 4 in.) in such a way that little visual experience was possible in the dim light used to carry out this procedure.

Each bird was given a number that was recorded on the box itself, as well as in our permanent records. The boxes, each containing its bird, were then placed in a still-air incubator, used as a brooder, and kept there until the birds were to be imprinted. After imprinting, each bird was automatically returned to its box, and the box was then transferred to a fourth incubator, also used as a brooder, and kept there until the bird was to be tested.

Imprinting Procedure. A certain number of hours after hatching, the young mallard was taken in its box from the incubator and placed in the runway of the apparatus. At this time the decoy was situated about 1 ft. away. By means of a cord, pulley, and clip arrangement the observer released the bird and removed the box. As the bird was released, the sound was turned on in the

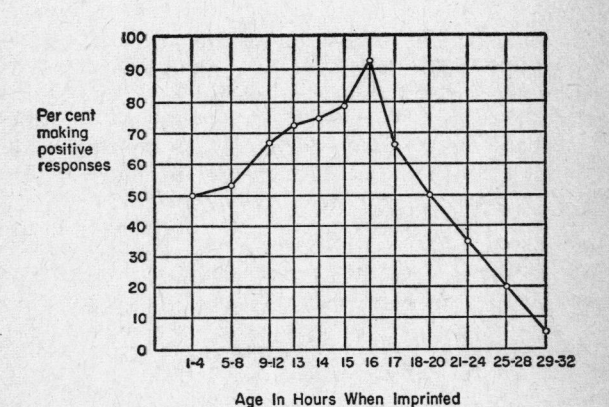

Fig. 1. Critical age for imprinting in mallards expressed as the per cent of positive responses.

Fig. 2. Critical age for imprinting in mallards expressed as the per cent of animals making perfect scores.

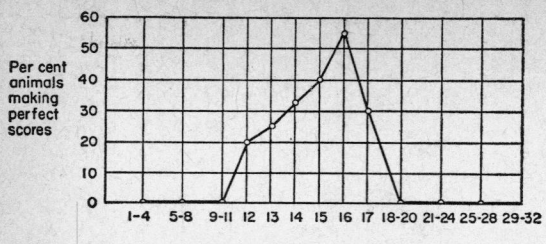

decoy model and, after a short interval, the decoy began to move about the circular runway. The sound used in the imprinting of the mallard ducklings was an arbitrarily chosen human rendition of "GOCK, gock, gock, gock, gock." The decoy sounded this call continually during the imprinting process. The duckling was allowed to remain in the apparatus for a specified amount of time while making a certain number of turns in the runway. At the end of the imprinting period, which was usually less than 1 hr., the duckling was automatically returned to its box and placed in an incubator until it would be tested at a later hour for imprinting strength.

Testing for Imprinting. Each duckling to be tested was mechanically released from its box halfway between 2 duck models placed 4 ft. apart. One of these was the male mallard model upon which the test duckling had been imprinted; the other was a female model that differed from the male only in its coloration. One minute was allowed for the duckling to make a decisive response to the silent models. At the end of this time, regardless of the nature of the duckling's response sound was turned on simultaneously with each of the models. The male model made the "GOCK" call upon which the duckling had been imprinted, while the female model gave the call of a mallard duck calling her young. The 4 test conditions following in immediate succession were: (1) both models stationary and silent; (2) both models stationary and calling; (3) male stationary and female moving, both calling; and (4) male stationary and silent, female moving and calling. Scores in percentage of positive responses were then recorded for each animal.

EXPERIMENT I
THE CRITICAL AGE FOR IMPRINTING IN MALLARDS

Ducklings were imprinted at various hours after hatching in an effort to determine the age at which an imprinting experience of 10 min. with a "following" response of about 150 to 200 ft. was maximally effective. The results were determined initially in 1953, but were substantiated and enlarged upon in 1954. Some imprinting appears possible almost immediately after hatching, but a maximum score is consistently made only by those ducklings imprinted in the 13- to 16-hr. group. This result is indicated in Figure 1.

Another way in which we can look at these data would be to consider only the number of animals in each age group (grouped by 4-hr. intervals) that make perfect scores, that is, that respond positively to all aspects of the test situation. When plotting the percentages for such "completely imprinted" animals, we find an even sharper peak, indicating that maximum imprinting is easiest in the mallard when imprinting occurs over a brief period at from 15 to 16 hr. after hatching. In our initial groups, no animal imprinted at less than 12 hr. or more than 16 hr. made a perfect score. Additional data obtained in 1954 indicate that the optimal age is closer to 16 hr., building gradually up to that point and then falling sharply after about 17 hr. The test results of the critical age for optimal imprinting are shown in Figure 2.

EXPERIMENT II
IMPRINTING STRENGTH AS A FUNCTION OF DISTANCE TRAVELED

In an effort to determine how long an imprinting experience must last to be maximally effective, we decided independently to vary the factors of time of exposure and the actual distance traveled by the duckling during the imprinting period. Since previous results had indicated that a 10-min. exposure period was sufficient to produce testable results, we decided to run a series of tests using varying distances but keeping the time constant at 10 min. We therefore used 1 circumference of the runway (12½ ft.) as a unit and ran groups of animals for 0, 1, 2, 4, and 8 turns. This resulted in imprinting experiences in which the ducklings moved about 1 ft., and 12½, 25, 50, and 100 ft., respectively. All ducklings were imprinted between 12 and 17 hr. of age in order to keep the variable of the critical period constant. The results showed that increasing the distance over which the duckling had to follow the imprinting object increased the imprinting strength. A leveling off of this effect appeared to occur after a distance of about 50 ft. These results are shown in Figure 3.

EXPERIMENT III
IMPRINTING STRENGTH AS A FUNCTION OF EXPOSURE TIME

In order to determine the effect of the length of the exposure time on imprinting strength, we chose a distance that could be traversed by ducklings in periods of time as short as 2, 10, and 30 min. Scores made by animals imprinted for these 3 time periods, while traveling a distance of 12½ ft., were essentially identical. There was also no significant difference between the scores of ducklings allowed to follow for a distance of 100 ft. during 10 min. and those allowed 30 min. to cover the same distance. Both of these results are shown in Figure 4. The results for 50 ft. are also shown. These scores fall between the ones for 12 and 100 ft.

DRUG EXPERIMENTS

The previously mentioned experiments show, first, that there is a well-defined maximum period when imprinting

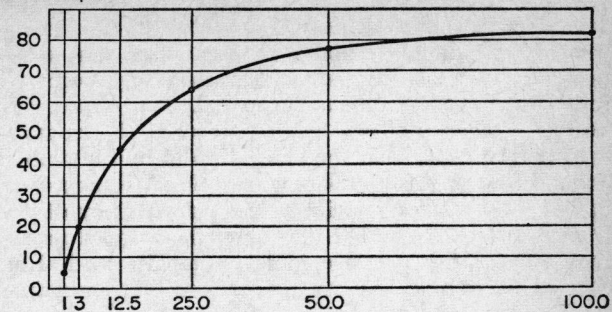

Fig. 3. Imprinting strength as a function of effort or the distance traveled.

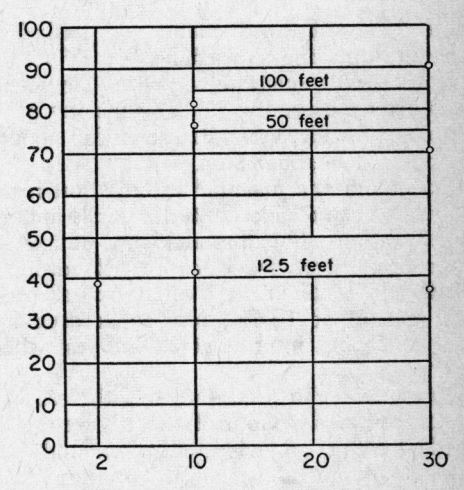

Fig. 4. Imprinting strength as a function of exposure time during the imprinting period.

can best take place and, second, that the strength of imprinting is related directly to the effort expended by the duckling in getting to or keeping up with the imprinting object. In addition, it should be mentioned that emotional responses on the part of the ducklings begin to appear when they are about 20 hr. old. This response is a fear or avoidance of any moving object in the environment. It is probable that the rapid drop in imprintability is coupled with this developing emotional response—a response that makes imprinting impossible. Almost 80 per cent of the 24-hr.-old ducklings show this fear response, and the percentage increases rapidly to 100 at about 32 hr. or older. To examine this aspect of imprinting, it seemed logical to reduce the emotional response by the use of a tranquilizing drug. Meprobamate was chosen because of evidence that it would reduce emotionality without markedly influencing motility or coordination. Preliminary experiments with dosages of 14 to 30 mg./kg. of body weight showed clearly that the emotionality of the duckling was markedly reduced. In fact, the duckling showed no fear of strange objects or persons, even though he was at an age when marked fear is normally a certainty. The effectiveness of meprobamate, introduced orally, was noticeable after about 20 min. and disappeared in about 5 hr.

To obtain the maximal information from this experiment, we then decided to test animals under the 4 following conditions: (1) drug at 12 hr., imprint at 24 hr., test when drug effect had worn off; (2) drug at 12 hr., imprint at 14 to 16 hr., test when drug effect had worn off; (3) imprint at 16 hr., test under drug later; and (4) drug at 24 hr., imprint at 26 hr., test when drug effect had worn off.

In general, the procedure was the same as that mentioned previously. Control animals were given ⅓ c.c. of distilled water, and chlorpromazine and Nembutal were used to obtain additional information. The results are shown in Table 1 below:

It is obvious that, while meprobamate reduces the fear, or emotional behavior, it also makes imprinting almost impossible. It does not, however, interfere with the ef-

TABLE 1

Per cent of positive responses made by ducklings under different conditions of testing and drug administration

	Control H$_2$O	Meprobamate 25 mg./kg.	Nembutal 5 mg./kg.	Chlorpromazine 15 mg./kg.
1. Drug at 12 hours, imprint at 24 hours	14	54	31	57
2. Drug at 12 hours, imprint at 14 to 16 hours	62	8	28	63
3. Imprint without drug at 16 hours, test under drug	61	65	61	58
4. Drug at 24 hours, imprint at 26 hours	19	17	16	59

fects of imprinting. This is clear from the results of test 3. Chlorpromazine apparently allows a high degree of imprinting under all conditions, whereas Nembutal reduces imprintability at all points except under the conditions of test 3.

CONCLUSIONS

From the data thus far presented, it appears that we might interpret the action of the drugs as follows. If we assume that meprobamate and chlorpromazine reduce metabolism, then we could expect the high imprinting scores at 24 hr. (test 1), because metabolism had been slowed and we had thus stretched out the imprinting or sensitive period. This did not occur when we used Nembutal or distilled water. The second point deals with the reduction of emotionality. In test 4 we had little evidence of emotionality in the meprobamate and the chlorpromazine group. This did occur in the control and in the Nembutal group. Thus far, the only way we can interpret this former result is to consider the finding of experiment II. Here we found that the strength of imprinting was a function of effort or of distance traveled. It may be that, since meprobamate is a muscle relaxant, these effects of meprobamate cut into the muscular tension or other afferent consequences and thus nullify the effectiveness of the imprinting experience. Since, under the same circumstances, we attain perfectly good imprinting in all cases with chlorpromazine, this notion becomes even more tenable. In an earlier paper, Hunt [15] stated some of these preliminary results and arrived at much the same conclusion in a personal communication. Further studies already in progress are continuing within this framework.

SUMMARY

Briefly, imprinting is an extremely rapid form of learning that can take place only during a very brief period in the early life of some organisms. Mallard ducklings show this effect maximally only between 12 and 17 hr. after hatching. This was expressed experimentally in the mallard ducklings by the rapidity with which they could learn to follow a moving object exposed to them during a brief period of time. The strength of the imprinting effect is directly related to the amount of muscular energy expended by the mallard in getting to, or in following, the object. The amount of exposure time is not relevant.

Using dosages of about 25 mg. of meprobamate per kg. of body weight, the following results have been obtained:

(1) Imprinting of mallards during the critical age (12 to 17 hr.) is almost impossible when the birds are under the influence of the drug. The animals are, however, quite active and behave normally.

(2) Animals imprinted at the critical age without the drug will show the response of following, even though they are tested for following under the standard dosage of meprobamate.

(3) Animals given a standard dose of meprobamate at 24 hr. cannot be imprinted at 26 hr., even though they do not show the fear and avoidance behavior ordinarily exhibited at that age.

(4) Meprobamate appears to extend the critical age for imprinting. Animals given meprobamate at 12 hr. can be imprinted fairly successfully at 24 hr. to 26 hr. when the effect of the drug has worn off.

These results are apparently in accord with the metabolism-lowering and muscle-relaxant effects of meprobamate.

REFERENCES

1. BEACH, F. A. AND J. JAYNES, 1954. Effects of early experience upon the behavior of animals. *Psychol. Bull.* 51: 239-263.
2. HEBB, D. O., 1949. *The Organization of Behavior.* Wiley, New York, N.Y.
3. CRAIG, W., 1908. The voices of pigeons regarded as a means of social control. *Am. J. Sociol.* 14: 86-100.
4. HEINROTH, O., 1910. Beitrage zur Biologie, namentlich Ethologie und Physiologie der Anatiden. *Verhandl. 5th Intern. Ornithol. Kongr.*: 589-702.
5. HEINROTH, O. AND M. HEINROTH, 1924-1933. *Die Vögel Mitteleuropas.* Lichterfelde, Berlin, Germany.
6. LORENZ, K., 1935. Der Kumpan in der Umwelt des Vogels. *J. Ornithol.* 83: 137-214, 289-413.
7. RAMSAY, A. O. AND F. H. HESS, 1954. A laboratory approach to the study of imprinting. *Wilson Bull.* 66: 196-206.
8. FABRICIUS, E., 1951. Zur Ethologie junger Anatiden. *Acta zool. fenn.* 68: 1-175.
9. RAMSAY, A. O., 1951. Familial recognition in domestic birds. *The Auk*, 68:1-16.
10. THORPE, W. H., 1944. Some problems of animal learning. *Proc. Linn. Soc. Lond.* 156: 70-83.
11. BAERENDS, G. P. AND J. M. BEAERENDS-VAN ROON, 1950. An introduction to the ethology of Cichlid fishes. *Behaviour suppl.* 1: 1-243.
12. GRABOWSKI, U., 1941. Prägung eines Jungschafs auf den Menschen. *Z. Tierpsychol.* 4: 326-329.
13. DARLING, F. F., 1938. *Wild Country.* Cambridge Univ. Press, London, England.

14. HEDIGER, H., 1950. *Wild Animals in Captivity*. Butterworth, London, England.
15. HUNT, H. F., 1956. Some effects of drugs on classical (type S) conditioning. *Ann. N.Y. Acad. Sci.* 65 (4): 258-267.

DISCUSSION OF THE PAPER

QUESTION: What route of administration was used?

E. H. Hess: The oral route. We found that in a very subdued blue light, to which the animals are relatively insensitive, we could get the material down very quickly with a medicine dropper. I should be a little afraid of injection with a needle although, at the same time, the animals were still aware of some contact and knew that something was stirring in the environment.

Julian Huxley (London, England): I do not think you gave us the figures of the strength of the imprinting. When the duck had a choice, how often did it follow the figure with which it had been imprinted? I should also like to ask whether you have not tried any other substitute objects.

Hinrod tried various substitute objects; within certain limits it is possible to substitute all kinds of curious things, and this, I think, is one of the strange things about imprinting—that the specificity of sign stimulus, so striking in many animal reactions, is largely, although not entirely, abolished.

E. H. Hess: The strength of imprinting depends on the effort expended. Also, if the imprinting has been done at the critical period, it is possible, under certain conditions, to make it one hundred per cent effective. We have worked with all kinds of substitute objects, but this would be more properly discussed in a meeting concerned with the problems of imprinting, and not with the effects of drugs on the imprinting or learning process.

J. Huxley: You said the imprinting always took place at an early age. I do not think this is necessarily so. In songbirds imprinting does not so take place. It occurs just when they are a year old or are coming into maturity. This may have some bearing on the fact that human beings are subject to a peculiar form of imprinting known as romantic love. It may take place when they reach puberty. The extremely important point brought out in this paper about imprinting is the fact that there is a critical period and that this period is usually quite brief.

Similar experiments that Scott has been doing on dogs at Bar Harbor have showed that there is a critical period when they can be trained and when they can become accustomed to human beings. If dogs are not tamed they remain wild forever. We have the same sort of thing in human beings, as Hess has said about mother love. Work done by Bulbey in England, and by Spitz in the United States, has shown that, if you deprive the child of the mother or a mother substitute during a critical period, the child will develop an apathy or a lack of moral sense.

I must say that I think this is one of the most interesting pieces of work done in the relationship of drugs and general biology, and I hope very much that it will be continued.

E. H. Hess: I simplified things a bit by saying that imprinting always occurs at an early age. I mentioned Hebb's statement. I think that in some respects he is quite wrong, because I agree with Lornez that there are probably periods in the lives of some animals during which certain kinds of social imprinting take place. It certainly occurs in the dog when he becomes sexually mature as when, territorially, for example, he may or may not team up with some pack and accept some leader. Of course the experiments by Scott show that, although very little handling is necessary, some human handling must occur between the age of four and seven weeks. If this does not happen the animal will never be a tamable dog. There are very important experiments that deal also with this general area.

10

An Attempt at Synthesis

NIKOLAAS TINBERGEN

This portion of the fifth chapter of Tinbergen's book, *The Study of Instinct* (copyright 1951 by Oxford University Press, Inc., reprinted by permission), presents his theory of the instinctive processes. The preceding chapters of the book contain a detailed account of his studies of birds and fish, with particular emphasis placed upon the activity of the stickleback fish. After marshalling his facts, the author then attempts to interpret them with a unified theory of behavior. This task raises for him the problem of the proper terminology to be used in referring to some of these processes.

RECAPITULATION

We have now arrived at a point where it is necessary to review our results in order to evaluate and appreciate their significance in relation to our main problem, that is, the problem of the causation of instinctive behavior.

The foregoing chapters have led to the following conclusions.

Instinctive behavior is dependent on external and internal causal factors. The external factors, or sensory stimuli, are of a much simpler nature than our knowledge of the potential capacities of the sense organs would make us expect. Yet they are not so simple as the word 'stimulus' would suggest, for the 'sign stimuli' have gestalt character, that is to say, they release configurational receptive processes. The various sign stimuli required for the release of an instinctive activity co-operate according to the rule of heterogeneous summation. These facts led us to the postulation of Innate Releasing Mechanisms, one of which is possessed by each separate reaction.

Apart from releasing stimuli, directing stimuli play a part, enabling or forcing the animal to orient itself in relation to the enivornment. The internal causal factors controlling, qualitatively and quantitatively, the motivation of the animal may be of three kinds: hormones, internal sensory stimuli, and, perhaps, intrinsic or automatic nervous impulses generated by the central nervous system itself. Instinctive 'reactions' are of varying degrees of complexity; even the simplest type, the 'fixed pattern,' depends on a system of muscle contractions which is of a configurational character.

These results are incomplete in more than one respect. First, the evidence is still very fragmentary, and the generalizations are still of a very tentative nature. Second, the work done thus far has been mainly analytical, and no attempt has yet been made to combine the separate conclusions into a picture of the causal structure underlying instinctive behaviour as a whole. We have, however, gained one thing: we are realizing more and more clearly that the physiological mechanisms underlying instinctive behaviour are much more complicated than we were able to see at the start. Previous attempts at synthesis, such as Pavlov's reflex theory and Loeb's tropism theory, now appear to be grotesque simplifications.

While thus realizing both the relative paucity of analytical data and the complexity of the causal structure, we will nevertheless venture to sketch, in rough outline, a synthetic picture of the organization of the partial problems within the main problem as a whole.

DIFFERENCES IN DEGREE OF COMPLEXITY OF 'REACTIONS'

So far I have been using the terms 'reactions,' 'motor response,' 'behaviour pattern,' 'movement' for muscle contractions of very different degrees of complexity. This fact is of paramount importance, and I will emphasize it by presenting some more instances.

As we have seen, the swimming of an eel is a relatively simple movement. In every somite there is alternating contraction of the longitudinal muscles of the right and the left half of the trunk. In addition, the pendulum movements of successive somites are slightly out of step, each somite contracting a short time after its predecessor. The result is the propagation of the well-known sinusoid contraction waves along the body axis. (Gray, 1936.)

The swimming movements of a fish like Labrus or Sargus, as described by von Holst (1935b, 1937), are more complex. The pectoral fins, moving back and forth in alternation, are also in step with the dorsal, caudal, and anal fins, each of which makes pendulum movements as well.

The movement of a male stickleback ventilating its eggs is of a similar type. The pectorals make pendulum movements alternately. This motion is directed forward, resulting in a water current from the fish to the nest. In order to counteract the backward push this exerts upon the fish, forward swimming movements of the tail are made in absolute synchronization with the rhythm of the pectorals.

Although locomotion might be considered merely an element of a 'reaction' in the sense in which I have been been using this term, the stickleback's ventilating movement is a complete reaction, responding in part to a chemical stimulus emanating from the nest.

The reaction of a gallinaceous chick to a flying bird of prey is, again, somewhat more complicated. It may consist of merely crouching, but often it consists of running to shelter provided by the mother or by vegetation, crouching, and continuously watching the predator's movements.

Finally, a male stickleback in reproductive condition responds to visual and temperature stimuli of a rather simple type by behaviour of a very complicated pattern: it settles on a territory, fights other males, starts to build a nest, courts females, and so on.

HIERARCHICAL ORGANIZATION

A closer study of these differences in complexity leads us to the conclusion that the mechanisms underlying these reactions are arranged in a hierarchical system, in which we must distinguish between various levels of integration.

The reproductive behaviour of the male stickleback may be taken as an example.

In spring, the gradual increase in length of day brings the males into a condition of increased reproductive motivation, which drives them to migrate into shallow fresh water. Here, as we have seen, a rise in temperature, together with a visual stimulus situation received from a suitable territory, releases the reproductive pattern as a whole. The male settles on the territory, its erythrophores expand, it reacts to strangers by fighting, and starts to build a nest. Now, whereas both nest-building and fighting depend on activation of the reproductive drive as a whole, no observer can predict which one of the two patterns will be shown at any given moment. Fighting, for instance, has to be released by a specific stimulus, viz. 'red male intruding into the territory.' Building is not released by this stimulus situation but depends on other stimuli. Thus these two activities, though both depend on activation of the reproductive drive as a whole, are also dependent on additional (external) factors. The influence of these latter factors is, however, restricted, they act upon either fighting or building, not on the reproductive drive as a whole.

Now the stimulus situation 'red male intruding,' while releasing the fighting drive, does not determine which one of the five types of fighting will be shown. This is determined by additional, still more specific stimuli. For instance, when the stranger bites, the owner of the teritory will bite in return; when the stranger threatens, the owner will threaten back; when the stranger flees, the owner will chase it, and so on.

Thus the effect of a stimulus situation on the animal may be of different kinds. The visual stimulus 'suitable territory' activates both fighting and nest-building, the visual situation 'red male in territory' is specific in releasing fighting, but it merely causes a general readiness to fight and does not determine the type of fighting. Which one of the five motor responses belonging to the fighting pattern will be shown depends on sign stimuli that are still more restricted in effect. The tactile stimulus 'male biting' releases one type of fighting, the visual stimulus 'male threatening' releases another type. The stimulus situations are not of an essentially different order in all these cases, but the results are. They belong to different levels of integration and, moreover, they are organized in a hierarchical system, like the staff organization of an army or other human organization (Fig. 1). The facts (1)

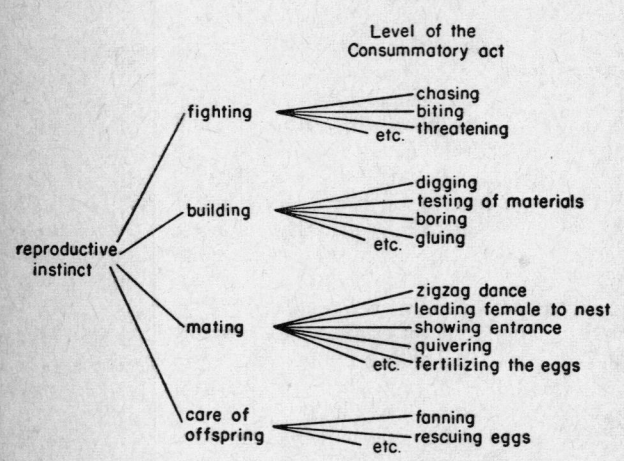

Fig. 1. The principle of hierarchical organization illustrated by the reproductive instinct of the male three-spined stickelback. After Tinbergen, 1942.

that at each of the levels an external stimulus can have a specific releasing influence and (2) that each reaction has its own motor pattern, mean that there is a hierarchical system of IRMs and of motor centres. So far as we can judge at present, each IRM is able to collect sensory impulses according to the rule of heterogeneous summation, and each motor centre controls a configurational pattern of muscle contractions.

The principle of hierarchical organization has been

tested in but three cases: the digger wasp *Ammophila campestris* (Baerends, 1941), the three-spined stickleback (Tinbergen, 1942), and the turkey (Räber, 1948), and although the principle is undoubtedly sound, nearly nothing is shown in detail about the way it works out in the various drives and in different species of animals. Before a more detailed discussion can be attempted, a closer consideration of motor responses is necessary.

APPETITIVE BEHAVIOUR AND CONSUMMATORY ACT

The activation of a centre of the lowest level usually, perhaps always, results in a relatively simple motor response: biting, chasing, threatening, etc., in the case of fighting in the stickleback; actual eating, actual escape, actual coition, etc., in other instincts. This type of response has been the object of our analysis in most of the cases treated in the preceding chapters. This is no accident; it is the natural outcome of the tendency to analyse which leads to a conscious or (more often) unconscious selection of relatively simple and stereotyped phenomena.

These relatively simple responses are, usually, the end of a bout of prolonged activity, and their performance seems to 'satisfy' the animal, that is to say, to bring about a sudden drop of motivation. This means that such an end-response consumes the specific impulses responsible for its activation. Fighting, eating, mating, 'playing the broken wing,' etc., are, as a rule, 'self-exhausting.' Craig (1918), in a most remarkable paper that has not received the attention it deserves, was the first to single out these elements of behaviour; he called them 'consummatory actions.' Lorenz (1937), realizing that they constitute the most characteristic components of instinctive behaviour, that is to say those components that can be most easily recognized by the form of the movement, called them *Instinkthandlungen*, thereby greatly narrowing the concept of instinctive act. This use of the term gives rise to continuous misunderstandings and hence should be dropped.

The centres of this lower type of movement rarely respond to the external stimulus situation alone. As a rule, they get their internal impulses from a superordinated centre. The activation of these higher centres may result either in a mere increase in readiness of the animal to react with one of a number of consummatory actions, or, more often, in a type of movement often called 'random movement,' 'exploratory behaviour,' 'seeking behaviour,' or the like. Contrary to the consummatory action it is not characterized by a stereotyped motor pattern, but rather by (1) its variability and plasticity, and (2) its purposiveness. The animal in which a major drive, like the hunting drive, the nest-building drive, the mating drive, is activated starts searching or exploratory excursions which last until a situation is found which provides the animal with the stimuli adequate for releasing the consummatory act.

As mentioned above, Craig recognized these two types of behaviour, viz. the variable striving behaviour and the rigid consummatory action; and, moreover, he saw their mutual relationships as components of instinctive behaviour as a whole. He called the introductory striving or searching phase 'appetitive behaviour' to stress the fact that the animal is striving to attain some end.

Appetitive behaviour may be a very simple introduction to a consummatory action, as in the case of a frog catching a prey; the preparatory taxis (turning towards the prey) is true purposive behaviour, and is continued or repeated until the prey is within range and in the median plane.

More complicated is the appetitive phase of feeding in a *Planaria* mounting a stream against a scent-loaded current.

Heinroth (1910) describes a still higher form of appetitive behaviour in mated ducks exploring the country for a nesting-hole.

In extreme cases the appetitive behaviour may be prolonged and highly adaptable, as in the migratory behaviour of animals.

It will be clear, therefore, that this distinction between appetitive behaviour and consummatory act separates the behaviour as a whole into two components of entirely different character. The consummatory act is relatively simple; at its most complex, it is a chain of reactions, each of which may be a simultaneous combination of a taxis and a fixed pattern. But appetitive behaviour is a true purposive activity, offering all the problems of plasticity, adaptiveness, and a complex integration that baffles the scientist in his study of behaviour as a whole. Appetitive behaviour is a conglomerate of many elements of very different order, of reflexes, of simple patterns like locomotion, of conditioned reactions, of 'insight' behaviour, and so on. As a result it is a true challenge to objective science, and therefore the discrimination between appetitive behaviour and consummatory act is but a first step of our analysis.

A consideration of the relationships between appetitive behaviour and consummatory act is important for our understanding of the nature of striving in animals. It is often stressed that animals are striving towards the attainment of a certain end or goal. Lorenz has pointed out not only that purposiveness, the striving towards an end, is typical only of appetitive behaviour and not of consummatory actions, but also that the end of purposive behaviour is not the attainment of an object or a situation itself, but the performance of the consummatory action, which is attained as a consequence of the animal's arrival at an external situation which provides the special sign stimuli releasing the consummatory act. Even psychologists who have watched hundreds of rats running a maze rarely realize that, strictly speaking, it is not the litter or the food the animal is striving towards, but the performance itself of the maternal activities or eating.

Holzapfel (1940) has shown that there is one apparent exception to this rule: appetitive behaviour may also lead to rest or sleep. As I hope to show further below, this exception is only apparent, because rest and sleep are true consummatory actions, dependent on activation of a centre exactly as with other consummatory actions.

Whereas the consummatory act seems to be dependent on the centres of the lowest level of instinctive behaviour, appetitive behaviour may be activated by centres of all the levels above that of the consummatory act. As has been pointed out by Baerends (1941), appetitive behaviour by no means always leads directly to the performance of a consummatory act. For instance, the hunting of a peregrine falcon usually begins with relatively random roaming around its hunting territory, visiting and exploring many different places miles apart. This first phase of appetitive behaviour may lead to different ways of catching prey, each dependent on special stimulation by a potential prey. It is continued until such a special stimulus situation is found; a flock of teal executing flight manoeuvres, a sick gull swimming apart from the flock, or even a running mouse. Each of these situations may cause the falcon to abandon its 'random' searching. But what follows then is not yet a consummatory action, but appetitive behaviour of a new, more specialized and more restricted kind. The flock of teal releases a series of sham attacks serving to isolate one or a few individuals from the main body of the flock. Only after this is achieved is the final swoop released, followed by capturing, killing, plucking, and eating, which is a relatively simple and stereotyped chain of consummatory acts. The sick gull may provoke the release of sham attacks tending to force it to fly up, if this fails the falcon may deftly pick it up from the water surface. A small mammal may release simple straightforward approach and subsequent capturing, etc. Thus we see that the generalized appetitive behaviour was continued until a special stimulus situation interrupted the random searching and released one of several possible and more specific types of appetitive behaviour. This in its turn was continued until the changing stimulus situation released the swoop, a still more specific type of appetitive behaviour, and this finally led to the chain of consummatory acts.

Baerends (1941) came to the same conclusion in his analysis of the behaviour of the digger wasp Ammophila campestris and probably the principle will be found to be generally applicable. It seems, therefore, that the centres of each level of the hierarchical system control a type of appetitive behaviour. This is more generalized in the higher levels and more restricted or more specialized in the lower levels. The transition from higher to lower, more specialized types of appetitive behaviour is brought about by special stimuli which alone are able to direct the impulses to one of the lower centres, or rather to allow them free passage to this lower centre. This stepwise descent of the activation from relatively higher to relatively lower centres eventually results in the stimulation of a centre or a series of centres of the level of the consummatory act, and here the impulse is finally used up.

This hypothesis of the mechanism of instinctive behaviour, though supported by relatively few and very fragmentary facts and still tentative therefore, seems to cover the reality better than any theory thus far advanced. Its concreteness gives it a higher heuristic value, and it is to be hoped that continued research in the near future will follow these lines and fill in, change, and adapt the sketchy frame.

NEUROPHYSIOLOGICAL FACTS

The Relatively Higher Levels

The hypothesis presented above, of a hierarchical system of nerve centres each of which has integrative functions of the 'collecting and redispatching' type has been developed on a foundation of facts of an indirect nature. If it is essentially right, it should be possible to trace these centres by applying neurophysiological methods. As I have said before, it must be considered as one of the greatest advantages of objective behaviour study that by using essentially the same method as other fields of physiology it gives rise to concrete problems that can be tackled by both the ethologist and the physiologist.

Now in recent times several facts have been brought to light which indicate that there is such a system of centres, at least in vertebrates.

I have already mentioned the fact that the work of Weiss, von Holst, Gray, Lissmann, and others proves that the spinal cord of fishes and maphibians must contain mechanisms controlling relatively simple types of co-ordinated movements, such as the locomotory contraction waves of the trunk muscles in fish or the locomotory rhythm of alternating contraction of leg muscles in axolotls. And although doubts have been raised concerning the absolute independence of these centres from external stimulation—doubts which have been discussed in Chapter III—the integrative, co-ordinative nature of the movements controlled by the motor centres is beyond doubt.

Other evidence of the same sort is given by the work of Adrian and Buytendijk (1931) on the respiratory centre in the medulla of fish.

However, all these facts concern the very lowest type of centre we have postulated, that of the consummatory action or, more probably still, that of its least complex component, the fixed pattern.

Now it seems to me to be of the highest importance that recently Hess (1943, 1944; Hess and Brügger, 1943, 1944; Brügger, 1943) has succeeded, by application of strictly local artificial stimuli, to elicit behaviour of a much higher level of integration. Hess succeeded in bringing minute electrodes into the diencephalon of intact cats. In this way he would apply weak stimuli to localized parts of the brain. By systematically probing the hypothalamic region he found areas where the application of a stimulus elicited the complete behaviour patterns of either fighting, eating, or sleep. His descriptions make it clear that all the elements of the pattern were not only present but were displayed in perfect co-ordination. Moreover, the response was initiated by genuine appetitive behaviour; the cat looked around and searched for a corner to go to sleep, it searched for food, etc. By combining this experiment with anatomical study the position of the centres of these patterns could be determined.

These results are of considerable interest in two respects.

First, Hess appears to have found the anatomical basis of the centres controlling instinctive patterns as a whole. A mere electric shock, surely a very simple type of stimulation, releases a complex pattern, an integrated whole of movements of the highest instinctive level. This lends support to our conclusion that somewhere between receptors and effectors there must be a mechanism that takes qualitatively different, configurational impulse-patterns coming from the receptors, combines them in a purely quantitative way, and takes care of redispatching them in re-integrative form so that a configurational movement results. Hess seems to have hit a station somewhere in this mechanism.

Second, the location of these centres is of interest in connexion with the findings about the functions of the spinal cord discussed above. While the spinal cord and the medulla seem to control only certain components of the instinctive patterns, the hypothalamus contains the highest centres concerned with instinctive behaviour. Our analysis of the hierarchical layout of behaviour patterns justifies the prediction that further research along the lines initiated by von Holst, Weiss, Gray, and Hess will lead to the discovery of a whole system of centres belonging to levels below the hypothalamic level as found by Hess, centres which are subordinate to the hypothalamic centres but which in their turn control centres lower still.

I should like to emphasize that this future work could only be done by workers who are fully acquainted with the instinctive behaviour as a whole and with its analysis, and at the same time are in command of neurophysiological methods and techniques. Our science is suffering from a serious lack of students with these qualifications, and it is an urgent task of ethologists and neurophysiologists to join efforts in the training of 'etho-physiologists.'

It is specially interesting that the hierarchical organization has not only been found in vertebrates but in insects as well. According to Baerends's results a wasp with a decentralized system of ventral ganglia and its relatively small 'brain' presents essentially the same picture as vertebrates.

Instinct and Instincts

The recognition of the hierarchical organization raises some problems of terminology. There is an enormous confusion around the use of the terms 'instinctive activity' or 'instinctive act.' Some authors maintain that instinctive behaviour is highly variable and adaptive in relation to a goal—in other words that it is purposive or directive—and that, because the goal remains constant while the movements, and hence the mechanisms employed, change, it is futile to attack instinctive behaviour with physiological methods. We have seen that this only applies to the appetitive part of behaviour, and moreover, that even in this purposive element of behaviour the number of possible movements and hence the number of available mechanisms is restricted. Other authors stress the rigidity, the stereotypy of instinctive behaviour.

Now it seems that the degree of variability depends entirely on the level considered. The centres of the higher levels do control purposive behaviour which is adaptive with regard to the mechanisms it employs to attain the end. The lower levels, however, give rise to increasingly simple and more stereotyped movements, until at the level of the consummatory act we have to do with an entirely rigid component, the fixed pattern, and a more or less variable component, the taxis, the variability of which, however, is entirely dependent on changes in the outer world. This seems to settle the controversy, the consummatory act is rigid, the higher patterns are purposive and adaptive. The dispute about whether 'instinctive behaviour' is rigid or adaptive has been founded on the implicit and entirely wrong assumption that there is only one type of instinctive activity.

The fact that the controversy is settled does not, of course, mean that the problem of purposiveness is solved. But the fact that even purposive behaviour appears to be dependent on quantitative activation of a centre and that it comes to an end whenever one of the lower centres has used the impulses shows that purposiveness as such is not a problem which cannot be studied by physiological methods. The fundamental problem is not to be found in the physiological mechanisms now responsible for purposive behaviour but in the history, the genesis of the species.

Returning now to our nomenclatural difficulty, the question naturally arises, What is to be called an instinctive act? Is it the pattern as a whole, or is it one of the partial patterns, or even, as Lorenz has proposed, the consummatory act? I would prefer to apply the name to all levels. For instance, reproductive behaviour in the male stickleback is, as a whole, an instinctive activity. But its component parts, nest-building and fighting, may also be called instinctive activities. A solution could be found by distinguishing instinctive acts of, for example, the first level, the second level, and so on. But here we meet with the additional difficulty that most probably the various major instinctive patterns of a species do not have the same number of levels. If we begin to count from the highest level, we would come to the absurd situation that various consummatory acts, though perhaps of the same degree of complexity, do not belong to the same level. If we begin at the level of the consummatory act, the major instincts would get different rank. This state of affairs renders it impossible to devise a universal nomenclature of instinctive behaviour as long as our knowledge is still in this fragmentary state.

It is of great importance for our understanding of instinctive behaviour as a whole to realize that the various instincts are not independent of each other. We have rejected the reflex hypothesis of behaviour and we have seen that each instinctive mechanism is constantly primed, that is to say, prepared to come into action. Such a system can only work because blocking mechanisms prevent the animal from performing continuous chaotic movements.

Now chaos is further prevented by another principle, viz. that of inhibition between centres of the same level. As a rule, an animal can scarcely do 'two things at a time.' Although there is a certain amount of synchronous activity of two instincts, this is only possible at low motivation, and, as a rule, the strong activation of instinctive behaviour of one kind prevents the functioning of another pattern. Thus an animal in which the sexual drive is strong is much less than normally susceptible to stimuli that normally release flight or eating. On the other hand, when flight is released, the thresholds of the reproductive and feeding activities are raised. The same relationship of mutual inhibition seems to exist between centres of lower levels. Intensive nest-building, for instance, renders the male stickleback much less susceptible than usual to stimuli normally releasing fighting, and vice versa.

Although the physiological basis of this inhibitory relationship will not be discussed here, it should be pointed out that its very existence has been the implicit origin of the distinction between various 'instincts' which has been made by numerous authors. So far, many authors who accepted a distinction between different instincts have defined them in terms of the goal or purpose they serve. A consideration of the neurophysiological relationships underlying instinct leads to a definition of 'an instinct' in which the responsible nervous centres and their mutual inhibition are also taken into account. It makes us realize that the purposiveness of any instinct is safeguarded by the fact that all the activities forming part of a purposive behaviour pattern aimed at the attainment of a certain goal depend on a common neurophysiological mechanism. Thus it is only natural that any definition of 'an instinct' should include not only an indication of the objective aim or purpose it is serving, but also an indication of the neurophysiological mechanisms. Because of the highly tentative character of my picture of these neurophysiological relationships it may seem a little early to attempt a definition of 'an instinct'; yet in my opinion, such an attempt could be of value for future research. I will tentatively define an instinct as a hierarchically organized nervous mechanism which is susceptible to certain priming, releasing and directing impulses of internal as well as of external origin, and which responds to these impulses of internal as well as of external origin, and which responds to these impulses by coordinated movements that contribute to the maintenance of the individual and the species.

For the same reason, it seems too early to attempt an enumeration of the various instincts to be found in animals and man. First, while we know that, in the cat, eating, fighting, and sleep must each be called a major instinct because each is dependent on the activation of a hypothalamic centre. There are patterns which almost certainly are equally dependent on a relatively high centre (e.g., escape, sexual behaviour, etc.) but of which nothing of the kind has yet been proved. Further, different species have different instincts. For instance, while many species have a parental instinct, others never take care of their offspring and hence probably do not have the corresponding neurophysiological mechanisms. However, such things are difficult to decide at present, because, for instance, it has been found that males of species in which the care of the young is exclusively an affair of the female can be brought to display the full maternal behaviour pattern by injecting them with prolactin. Though this example concerns individuals of the same species, we could not reject a priori the possibility that, for instance, a species might lack a certain instinct because, having lost it relatively recently, it retained the nervous mechanism but not the required motivational mechanism. So long as we know nothing about such things, it would be as well to refrain from generalizations.

However, it is possible to point out some inconsistencies in the present views on instincts to be found in the literature. Contrary to current views, there is, in my opinion, no 'social instinct' in our sense. There are no special activities to be called 'social' that are not part of some instinct. There is no such thing as the activation of a system of centres controlling social activities. An animal is called social when it strives to be in the neighbourhood of fellow members of its species when performing some, or all, of its instinctive activities. In other words, when these instincts are active, the fellow member of the species is part of the adequate stimulus situation which the animal tries to find through its appetitive behaviour. In some species all instincts, even the reproductive instinct and the instinct of sleep, have social aspects. In many other species the social aspect, while present in feeding or in all non-reproductive instincts, is absent from the reproductive instinct. This is especially obvious in many fishes and birds. In many amphibians the situation is just the reverse. Further, in many species there are differences of degree, or even of quality, between the social elements of different instincts. For instance, in herring gulls there is a tendency to nest in colonies. But in mating and nest-building there is only a weak social tendency, limited to the fact that individuals select their nesting site in the neighbourhood of an existing colony. Attacking a predator, one of the other sub-instincts of the reproductive instinct, is a much more social affair.

There is no instinct for the selection of the environment, no *Funktionskreis des Milieus* as von Uexküll (1921) claims. Here again reactions to habitat are parts of the reproductive instinct or of other instincts.

There is, however, an instinct of sleep. Sleep is a readily recognizable, though simple behaviour pattern and has a corresponding appetitive behaviour pattern; further, it is dependent on the activation of a centre. Moreover, sleep can appear as a displacement activity (see following paragraph in this book), a property found in true instinctive patterns only.

There is, further, an instinct of comfort, or rather of care of the surface of the body.

There is not one instinct of combat. There are several sub-instincts of fighting. The most common type of fighting is sexual fighting, which is part of the reproductive pattern. Sexual fighting has to be distinguished from defence against a predator, for it has a different IRM and, often, a different motor pattern.

11

The Inheritance of Behaviour: Behavioural Differences in Fifteen Mouse Strains

WILLIAM R. THOMPSON

This article originally appeared in the *Canadian Journal of Psychology*, 1953, Vol. 7, No. 4.

As Hall has pointed out in a recent review of the literature [12], a science of psychogenetics is as yet more of a promise than an actuality, and such work as has been done in it has been fragmentary and often based on inadequate methodology. Consequently, it is highly desirable that there be initiated a programme of research which takes cognizance of the failings of previous studies and starts off on a firm empirical foundation.

Two main techniques have been used in approaching the problem. One has been the method of selection. By interbreeding only the extremes in each generation, a number of investigators have produced strains of rats which are widely separated in "maze-brightness" [13, 16, 25, 26], emotionality [10], and activity [18]. The fact that such strains can be bred indicates that these traits definitely depend upon heredity. But the manner in which they are genetically transmitted is still unknown. Thus Tryon [26], for example, made crosses between his "bright" and "dull" animals, but since the variability of his F1 cross was as great as that of his F2, he was unable to undertake a genetic analysis. Similarly, Brody [2] made several crosses (F1, F2, and backcrosses) in the twenty-second and twenty-third generations of Rundquist's active and inactive strains. Although she concluded that the character of "inactivity" is transmitted by a single "inhibitor" gene, dominant in males and recessive in females, her results do not justify such a simplified interpretation, as Hall has remarked [12]. Hall, in an unpublished study [12], crossed his emotional and non-emotional rats, but obtained considerable heterogeneity in the F1. Kuppasawny [16] has theorized that general mental ability is determined not by a single factor or by multiple factors, but rather by the entire set of parental genes handed down in a given combination. He has no incisive evidence from his experimental work to support such a hypothesis.

In general, then, selection studies have contributed very little to our understanding of how behaviour is inherited. This has been owing to two main difficulties. First, close inbreeding has not been carried on sufficiently long to produce genetically pure strains. As a result, any cross made is bound to be so variable as to preclude the possibility of further analysis. Secondly, the trait for which selection is made is often highly complex, and may represent the interaction of a hierarchy of related characters. Such was the case with Tryon's strains, as shown by Searle [22]. This being so, it would seem essential to deal as far as possible with unitary traits, and to eliminate between the strains being bred any differences other than the one being specifically studied [25].

A second approach to the genetics of behaviour has been by the use of stock already known to be genetically homogeneous. By starting with pure strains one of the difficulties stated above is immediately eliminated. Yerkes [28], Coburn [3], Stone [24], Dawson [4], and Lindzey [17] have shown systematic differences in emotionality between various mouse and rat strains, but they did not pursue the matter far enough to gain any knowledge of the genetic basis of this trait. The studies of Bagg [1], Sadovnokova-Koltzova [19], and Vicari [27], dealing with maze-learning in different mouse and rat strains, showed considerable promise and deserved to be followed up. Unfortunately, they were not. From a genetic standpoint, the most profitable studies have been those initiated by Hall [11], and continued by Fuller and others [6, 7, 8], on the inheritance of audiogenic seizures in the mouse. These serve as a case in point, indicating the level of sophistication that can be attained in the field of psychogenetics. From a psychological standpoint, however, this work is of less importance. What is obviously needed is a thorough investigation of the normal psychological characteristics of some of the eighty-odd available mouse strains, followed by appropriate crosses and a genetic analysis.

The present experiment is the first step in such a programme. Specifically its purpose is the examination of food-drive, emotionality, and exploratory activity in fifteen mouse strains. These three parameters were chosen for two reasons: first, they are fundamental to many more complex types of behaviour; and secondly, they are measured with reasonable simplicity and with a minimum of handling of the animals.

THE EXPERIMENT

Animals

Samples of 20 animals (10 males, 10 females) from the following 14 inbred mouse strains were used in the experiment: C57BL/6, C57BL/10, C57BR/a, DBA/1, DBA/2, AKR, AK/e, A/C1, BALB/c, ND, C3H, TC3H, LP, BDP. These are described fully elsewhere [23]. The hybrid strain "obese" was also used. All animals had been reared under ostensibly identical conditions in the Jackson Laboratory colony. They were between 70 and 90 days of age at the time of testing.

Test 1. Food-drive and Emotionality

Apparatus. A modified Hall open-field test was used in this part of the experiment. It consisted simply of a standard mouse shipping-box (approximately 12 by 24 in.) with wire mesh top. In the centre of the box, on a sheet of paper, was placed a small glass dish containing 10 gm. of dry Purina mash mixed with milk powder.

Procedure. Ten boxes were used, thus allowing ten animals to be tested simultaneously. Each animal was put on a reduced ration of food, determined as follows: the mean weight of the animals was calculated, this being approximately 20 gm. Each animal was given daily one gm. of Purina checkers per 20 gm. of body weight during the six days of the test. Twenty-three hours after the mice had first been put on this ration, they were taken to the experimental room, and each put in one of the testing-boxes. They were allowed to eat and explore for ten minutes. At the end of this period, each was removed and returned to its living-cage in which it was given its daily ration of food. This procedure was repeated for the next five days. The amount of food consumed by an animal during each 10-minute test was determined by weighing the food in the dish before and after test. Since the amount of food that can be consumed by a mouse in ten minutes is not very large, a scale accurate to one-hundredth of a gram was used.

Defecation was used as a measure of emotionality, the scale being based on the frequency with which animals in a particular strain defecated over the six days.

Results. First, the total amounts of food eaten by each mouse of each strain over the six days of testing were compared. A rough plot made of these totals showed that they were heavily skewed positively. Consequently, for purposes of computation, they were normalized. An analysis of variance was then calculated on the transformed scores, with strains and sex as variables.[1] High significance was obtained between strains ($F = 9.32$, $p < .001$) but none between sexes. The interaction was not significant. Using the error (within) variance of this analysis, t tests were then made between each strain and every other one. The results of these tests are presented in Table I. It is clear that wide differences exist between the different strains in strength of food-drive. Out of 105 possible com-

---

[1] It should be mentioned that in both experiments the variances within strains were unequal, as shown by L tests for homogeneity (Experiment 1, $L = .83$, $p < .01$; Experiment 2, $L = .84$, $p < .01$). However, since the Fs were large in both cases, it is unlikely that the conclusions drawn from the analyses are seriously affected.

parisons, 60 were significantly different. However, only the highest and lowest strains showed a complete absence of overlap in their scores.

TABLE I

Mean grams of food eaten by fifteen mouse strains over six days, and the p values of differences between them

No.	Strain	Mean Gm. Eaten	P VALUES OF DIFFERENCES* .05-.01	.01-.001
1	TC3H	204	> 6	7-15
2	AKR	199	>	7-15
3	C3H	183	> 7	8-15
4	DBA/1	176	> 7-9	10-15
5	ND	171	> 7-10	11-15
6	C57BL/6	162	>10-11	12-15
7	AK/e	131	>13-15	
8	C57BR/a	128	>13-15	
9	LP	124	>13-15	
10	DBA/2	121	>13-15	
11	C57BL/10	116		
12	BALB/c	99		
13	Ob	82		
14	BDP	82		
15	A/C1	80		

* Read, for example, as follows: No. 1, Strain TC3H has a mean of 204 gm., significantly greater than Strains No. 6 ($p = .05-.01$) and Nos. 7 to 15 $p = .01-.001$).

The second point of interest was the change in strength of food-drive from the first to the last day. The amounts eaten by each strain were plotted as a function of time and then compared. On inspection, there were found to be marked differences between strains in this respect. Since the irregularity of the curves did not permit an exact analysis of their slopes, the gain from the first three to the last three days was computed for each strain to allow a gross comparison to be made. These figures are presented in Table II. By comparing them with the scores in Table I, it can be seen that they bear little relation to total amounts eaten over all six days together.

Thirdly, a comparison was made between the fifteen strains with respect to emotionality as measured by frequency of defecation over the six days of testing. The percentages of animals of each strain defecating during the six days are presented in Table III. A chi square computed on these data was found to be significant ($p < .001$).

TABLE II

*Gains in eating amount from first to second half of test 1
(Sessions 4-6/Sessions 1-3)*

Strain	Gain in gm.	Strain	Gain gm.	Strain	Gain in gm.
BALB/C	21.40	TC3H	2.05	AKR	1.66
C57/BRa	3.41	AC1	2.01	BDP	1.59
LP	3.18	C57/10	1.97	Ob	1.52
AK/e	2.44	C57/6	1.96	C3H	1.26
ND	2.20	DBA2	1.86	DBA1	.95

As might be expected, food-drive and emotionality were inversely related. The fifteen strains were put in rank order for each of these two variables, and a rank-order correlation run. The coefficient obtained was -0.796 which is significant ($p < .001$).

TABLE III

*Percentage of mice in each of fifteen strains
defecating during six 10-minute tests*

Strain	%	Strain	%	Strain	%
AK/e	96	A/C1	78	C3H	52
BDP	85	DBA/2	70	C57BL/6	40
Ob	83	C57BR/a	66	AKR	34
LP	82	C57BL/10	58	ND	27
BALB/c	82	DBA/2	57	TC3H	11

Test 2. Exploratory Activity

Apparatus. A square enclosure 30 by 30 by 3¾ in. with a wire mesh top was used in this test. The floor was painted gray, the walls and wire top a flat black. The floor was divided by pencil lines into 36 small squares, each 5 by 5 in. At the base of every other square was placed a single unit barrier of corresponding length and height, there being 15 of these in all. At one corner of and leading into the enclosure was a small starting box in which each animal was placed at the start of a test. A diagram of the floor-plan is shown in Figure 1.

Procedure. Each mouse was placed in the starting compartment and given 10 minutes to explore the enclosure. A record was taken of the number of lines transversed by each mouse, this being used as an index of strength of exploratory drive. For purposes of determining the reliability of the test, ten mice (five males, five females) from each strain were run twice, on consecutive days.

Results. An analysis of variance was computed on the data, giving the following results: the variance of strain means was significant ($F = 11.71$, $p < .001$). No sex difference appeared, and the interaction was not significant. Again, using the error term of this analysis, t tests were made between each strain and every other strain. The results are presented in Table IV. Of the 105 possible comparisons, 68 were found to be significant. There were no overlap between the highest and the two

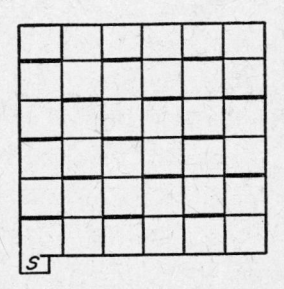

Fig. 1. Groundplan of the apparatus used in measuring exploratory activity. Thick lines represent barriers.

lowest strains, nor between the second two highest and the lowest.

The reliability of the test for the whole group of mice which were run twice ($N = 150$) was found to be 0.925, ($p < .001$). Within each strain, it varied somewhat, being above 0.900 in five cases, above 0.800 in six cases, and below 0.600 and not significant in four cases.

The Relationship between Test 1 and Test 2

It seems plausible that there would be some relationship, either negative or positive, between the amount of food eaten in Test 1 and the strength of exploratory drive in Test 2. For example, one might argue that timidity or lack of it in an animal would interfere or facilitate performance in both tests. On the other hand, a strong tendency to explore might well be expected to

TABLE IV

Mean amount of exploratory activity shown by each of fifteen mouse strains, and the p values of differences between them

No.	Strain	Mean score	P VALUE OF DIFFERENCES* .05-.01	.01-.001
1	C57BR/a	459	> 3-4	5-15
2	C57BL/6	361	> 7-9	10-15
3	C57BL/10	359	> 7-9	10-15
4	DBA/1	334	> 8-10	11-15
5	ND	308	> 8-11	12-15
6	BDP	286	>10-12	13-15
7	DBA/2	253	>11-13	14-15
8	LP	194	>13-15	
9	AKR	188	>13-15	
10	C3H	177	>13-15	
11	Ob.	149	>15	
12	TC3H	117		
13	BALB/c	74		
14	AK/e	60		
15	A/C1	20		

* Read as in Table I.

draw an animal's attention away from food, and so produce a negative relationship between the two tests. In fact, neither of these possibilities is supported by the data. A correlation between the two tests gave a rank-order coefficient of 0.150 which is not significant. Consequently, they may be considered to be independent.

DISCUSSION

To summarize the results, significant differences in food-drive, emotionality, and exploratory activity were found between a number of the fifteen mouse strains tested. Since all strains were reared in ostensibly identical conditions, these differences may be considered to have a genetic basis.

Contrary to the observations of Keeler [14, 15], no definite relationship appeared between the behavioural traits studied and coat-colour or other morphological characteristics. On a gross observational level, black, brown, and gray mice tended to be wilder and harder to handle than most albinos, agoutis, and piebalds. But there was little indication that coat-colour genes might usefully serve as markers for functional traits.

Now, although some of the strains studied were clearly different from each other, there was found to be, nevertheless, great variability within each one. This often resulted in overlap between stocks whose mean scores were widely separated. With complex psychological traits which probably depend on multiple factors, variability is perhaps to be expected, and, as Dobzhansky [5] has pointed out, the designation "hereditary" need not be restricted to characters which show a certain constancy of expression. Such traits as aggressiveness and dominance, for example, while having a genetic basis, can readily be altered by training [9]. From the standpoint of analysis, of course, it is more satisfactory to deal with traits which do not vary a great deal within homogeneous stocks, and are fairly resistant to environmental influences. But in the field of behaviour, such traits may be few and far between. Consequently, if psychogenetics is to make any progress, it will be necessary to examine the sources of variability and find methods of reducing it to a minimum.

Obviously, any variability that appears within a given population will depend on two main causes. The first is the genetic background of the individuals making up the population. Since the strains used in the present experiment were all inbred (the criterion for an inbred strain being 20 consecutive brother-sister matings) it is probably that genetic variation was minimal within each strain. None the less, there may have been some. Complete genetic homogeneity is reached by inbreeding only in the limit; furthermore, minor mutations may have occurred spontaneously from time to time. The effects of such slight genetic variation on behavioural phenotypes are difficult to determine, but sometimes they may be important. By way of illustration, Scott [20] has shown that under weak illumination *drosophila* will crawl to or away from a light, depending upon the possession of red or white eyes, a difference conditioned by a single gene. Under threshold conditions, in other words, a slight structural difference may have a greatly magnified effect at the behavioural level [21]. Similarly, with the naive animals used in the present experiment, it is possible that slight environmental disturbances (noises, movements, etc.) may have interacted with minor genetic differences so as to produce considerable variation in behaviour.

The second main cause of variation is the environment. Conditions of testing were naturally made as constant as possible for all subjects, but it is not unlikely that conditions of rearing varied somewhat. Slight differences in handling, maternal care, position of living-box in relation to light, and other such factors, may have produced lasting effects.

Now, since some of the most highly inbred stocks showed as much variability as less inbred ones, it is doubtful if further inbreeding would result in appreciably greater within-strain homogeneity. Also, as we have pointed out, the testing-environment of the subjects was held constant and thus could not have been responsible for much of the variance. Consequently, it is probable that the early environment of the subjects was the most important source of variation. This being so, it would seem desirable to control it by raising all animals under as similar conditions as possible. Perhaps the best method of doing this would be by rearing all subjects in a "free" environment, providing a wide variety of stimulation from a very early age. This should result in a heightened threshold of reactivity in the animals, and as a consequence the effects of some unusual stimulus or experience on any particular animal should be minimized. There is no reason to suppose, of course, that strain differences obtained with naive animals will necessarily hold after such treatment. But new differences which are more stable and less variable within strains might well appear, and these would be of equal interest. Furthermore, they should be more easy to analyse genetically.

Variability is not the only problem in this area of research. Another is that of choosing simple and unitary traits. To a large extent, this is a matter of trial and error. However, if the assumption is made that the more unitary the trait is, the more simple will be its genic basis, then an independent check will be available on the suitability of any one chosen for examination.

From a genetic analysis of simple behavioural characters, psychogenetics should eventually be able to predict the manner of transmission of more complex traits compounded of several simple ones, and then check the prediction against empirical data. Such an undertaking is, however, a long way from fulfilment. Before any real progress can be made, a great deal of work will have to be done. The experiment presented above represents an initial step in such a programme.

SUMMARY

The above experiment was a preliminary step in a programme of research designed to study the genetics of behaviour in mice. Specifically, an examination was made of three behavioural traits, food-drive, emotionality, and exploratory activity, in 14 different inbred mouse strains, and one hybrid strain. Significant differences in each of these characteristics were found between a number of the strains tested, indicating that they have a genetic basis. Several problems in this area of research were discussed briefly.

REFERENCES

1. BAGG, H. J. "Individual Differences and Family Resemblances in Animal Behavior" (*American Naturalist*, 50, 1916, 222-36).
2. BRODY, E. G. "Genetic Basis of Spontaneous Activity in the Albino Rat" (*Comparative Psychology Monographs*, 17, 1942, no. 5).
3. COBURN, C. A. "Heredity of Wildness and Savageness in Mice" (*Behavior Monographs*, 4, 1922, no. 5, 1-71).
4. DAWSON, W. M. "Inheritance of Wildness and Tameness in Mice" (*Genetics*, 17, 1932, 296-326).
5. DOBZHANSKY, T. "What is Heredity?" (*Science*, 100, 1944, 406).
6. FULLER, J. L. "Gene Mechanisms and Behavior" (*American Naturalist*, 85, 1951, 145-57).
7. FULLER, J. L., EASLER, CLARICE, AND SMITH, MARY E. "Inheritance of Audiogenic Seizure Susceptibility in the Mouse" (*Genetics*, 35, 1950, 622-32).
8. FULLER, J. L. AND WILLIAMS, ELIZABETH. "Gene-Controlled Time Constants in Convulsive Behavior" (*Proceedings of the National Academy of Science*, 37, 1951, 349-56).
9. GINSBURG, B., AND ALLEE, W. C. "Some Effects of Conditioning on Social Dominance and Subordination in Inbred Strains of Mice" (*Physiological Zoology*, 15, 1942, 485-506).
10. HALL, C. S. "The Inheritance of Emotionality" (*Sigma Xi Quarterly*, 26, 1938, 17-27).
11. ———— "Genetic Differences in Fatal Audiogenic Seizures between Two Inbred Strains of House Mice" (*Journal of Heredity*, 38, 1947, 2-6).
12. ————"The Genetics of Behavior" (in S. S. STEVENS, ed., *Handbook of Experimental Psychology*, New York: Wiley, 1951, 304-29).

13. Heron, W. T. "The Inheritance of Maze Learning Ability in Rats" (*Journal of Comparative Psychology*, 19, 1935, 77-89).
14. Keeler, C. E. "Coat Color, Physique, and Temperament: Materials for the Synthesis of Hereditary Behavior Trends in the Lower Mammals and Man" (*Journal of Heredity*, 38, 1947, 271-7).
15. ——— "Materials for the Synthesis of Hereditary Behavior Trends in Mammals" (*Journal of Comparative Physiological Psychology*, 41, 1948, 75-81).
16. Kuppusawny, B. "Laws of Heredity in Relation to General Mental Ability" (*Journal of General Psychology*, 36, 1947, 29-43).
17. Lindzey, G. "Emotionality and Audiogenic Seizure Susceptibility in Five Inbred Strains of Mice" (*Journal of Comparative Physiological Psychology*, 44, 1951, 389-93).
18. Rundquist, E. A. "Inheritance of Spontaneous Activity in Rats" (*Journal of Comparative Psychology*, 16, 1933, 415-38).
19. Sadovnikova-Koltzova, Mary P. "Genetic Analysis of Temperament in Rats" (*Journal of Experimental Zoology*, 45, 1926, 301-18).
20. Scott, J. P. "Effects of Single Genes on the Behavior of Drosophila" (*American Naturalist*, 77, 1943, 184-90).
21. ——— "The Magnification of Differences by a Threshold" (*Science*, 100, 1944, 659-70).
22. Searle, L. V. "The Organization of Hereditary Maze Brightness and Maze Dullness" (*Genetic Psychology Monographs*, 39, 1949, 279-325).
23. Standardized Nomenclature for Inbred Strains of Mice. The Committee on Standardized Nomenclature for Inbred Strains of Mice (Cancer Research, 12, 1952, 602-13).
24. Stone, C. P. "Wildness and Savageness in Rats" (in K. S. Lashley, ed., *Studies in the Dynamics of Behavior*, Chicago: University of Chicago Press, 1932).
25. Thompson, W. R., and Bindra, D. "Motivational and Emotional Characteristics of Bright and Dull

Rats" (*Canadian Journal of Psychology*, 6, 1952, 116-22).
26. TRYON, R. C. "Genetic Differences in Maze Learning Ability in Rats" (Yearbook of the National Society for the Study of Education, 39 (L) 1940, 111-19).
27. VICARI, E. M. "Mode of Inheritance of Reaction Time and Degrees of Learning in Mice" (*Journal of Experimental Zoology*, 54, 1929, 31-88).
28. YERKES, R. M., "The Heredity of Savageness and Wildness in Rats" (*Journal of Animal Behavior*, 3, 1913, 286-96).

12

Genetic Differences in Dogs: A Case of Magnification by Thresholds and by Habit Formations

JOHN P. SCOTT AND MARGARET S. CHARLES

This article originally appeared in the *Journal of Genetic Psychology*, 1954, Vol. 84, pp. 175-188.

The test data reported here comprise part of a long-time research program on genetics and the social behavior of dogs, and concern differences between breed populations. The work is financed by the Rockefeller Foundation.

A. INTRODUCTION

Some years ago [7] it was pointed out that although hereditary differences in behavior were often small and insignificant, these differences could be magnified by thresholds in various ways so that very large differences could be obtained under special conditions.

Two of these situations are illustrated in Figure 1. In the first of these, two individuals, A and B, have slightly different thresholds of response which are genetically determined, but the same upper limit of response. Near the upper limit they show very small differences, but if a stimulus is set between the two thresholds, an all-or-none difference in response is obtained. This situation apparently applies to a case where large differences in response to light and vibration were obtained with stocks of fruit flies [6], and also to the more highly social situation involving differences in the behavior of dogs which is described in this paper.

In the second case (Figure 1b . . .), two individuals are represented as having the same threshold, but a

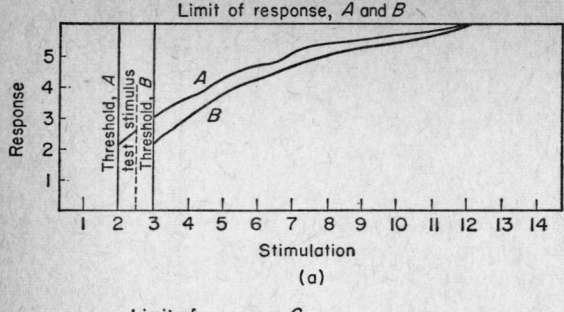

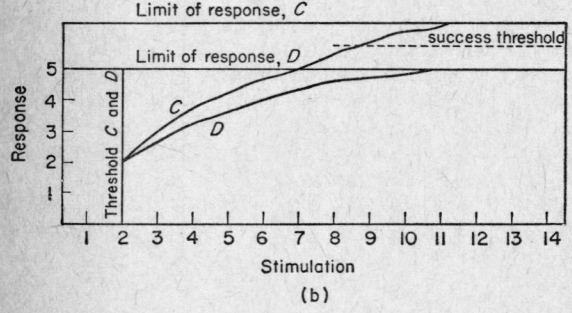

Fig. 1. Graphic representation of the magnification of genetic differences by thresholds.

(a) Above their respective thesholds of stimulation individuals A and B, which have the same upper limit of response, show a response difference of only one unit, this decreasing rapidly as the response limit is approached. However, if a test stimulus is applied between values 2 and 3, which correspond to the thresholds of the two individuals, there is an absolute difference between response and no response. In (b) is shown the theoretical situation in which the stimulus threshold is the same for both individuals, but the upper limit of response is different. The maximum difference in response is only one unit, but if a threshold of successful adjustment is set between the two upper limits the result will be an absolute difference between failure and success. This is the kind of situation produced by so-called "power tests."

different response rate and upper limit of response, which are genetically determined. Under most conditions the observed differences in behavior are small, but grow larger as the upper limit is approached. If a threshold of success or failure is set between the two upper limits of response, an all-or-none difference can be obtained. This is the sort of situation which may be set in certain competitive games and in the so-called "power tests" of intelligence and performance. Of course, an actual case might involve both types of genetic differences.

An interesting and more complicated case of the first type may be found in connection with agonistic behavior of mammals. When an animal is attacked he has three principal ways of adapting to the situation: to fight back, to run away, or to remain passive. Which of these responses is chosen depends largely upon strength of stimulation. A mild attack will cause an animal to fight back whereas a very severe one may cause him to adopt a completely passive attitude [8]. If animals have different genetically determined thresholds for stimulation it might be expected that a standard stimulation could cause one kind of animal to act passively and another to react with escape behavior or some form of mild or severe fighting.

This kind of interpretation appears to describe the results of a test situation in dogs in which an attempt was made to train puppies to stand still on the scales while being weighed. The methods used resulted in some animals becoming passive while others became more active, showing either escape behavior or playful aggressiveness.

The case is also interesting because the original differences observed became more definite and consistent as training proceeded. Apparently the original genetic differences, which probably act by producing different thresholds of stimulation, were still further magnified by habit formation, an effect which may be explained as follows. A very mild sort of manual control was used so that either passivity or playful fighting was possible as an adjustment to the situation. If there should be an hereditary tendency in an individual for one of these reactions to occur more frequently than another because of the proximity of a threshold, habit formation would tend to fix the most frequent response. Two genetically different individuals may at first show considerable overlap in their behavior but, after exposure to the same training situation, begin to show consistent differences. Thus we have still another way in which originally small genetic differences may be magnified. (For graphic illustrations of this effect, see later figures.)

This is an apparently paradoxical result which occurs fairly frequently in experiments with animals whose heredity is known. A priori, one would expect that young, naive animals would show greater genetic differences in behavior than older and more experienced individuals. Actually, the behavior of naive animals is usually quite variable and it is only after considerable training that such animals begin to behave consistently and clear-cut differences begin to appear.

B. METHODS AND POPULATIONS

These data were gathered as one part of the long-time experiment on genetics and the social behavior of dogs which is being carried out at the Jackson Laboratory [9, 10, 11]. The dogs are raised as much as possible under the same environmental conditions, and during the first 16 weeks of life each litter is raised in a large nursery room, 18 x 13 feet in size. Once each week the animals are weighed in order to check on their health and growth and it was in connection with this procedure that these data were obtained.

The weighing is done inside the room with the scales placed on the nestbox. The puppy is first picked up by a handler and its heart rate taken by means of a stethoscope for 15 seconds. It is then placed upon a platform scale and weighed, being gently restrained with the hands if it tries to get off. Ordinarily no talking is done and sudden movements are avoided. An observer, sitting nearby, rates the amount of activity on the scale during a period of one minute. A rating of *quiet* means that the animal does not shift its feet after being placed on the scale although it may change its position; e.g., from sitting to lying. A rating of *partially active* means that the dog was seen to shift its feet at some time during the one-minute period, while a rating of *active* means that the dog is constantly shifting its feet, never being quiet as long as five seconds consecutively.

An experiment on observer reliability was done with this test, ratings being made by both the handler and observer. A tetrachoric correlation coefficient was estimated on the basis of reducing the ratings to two classes, and this yielded a coefficient of reliability of .96. The ratings disagreed on 14 out of 54 ratings but in no case was there a difference of more than one point in the scale. The observer consistently rated animals as more quiet than did the handler. After a conference it was discovered that the cause of disagreement was a difference in interpreting the rating scale, which could be easily corrected. The ratings used are therefore those of the one observer, and may be considered as artificial thresholds set by the observer on the basis of time.

The reliability of successive observations was tested by comparing the ratings at 15 and 16 weeks. The scale was reduced to two categories, first by adding the "quiet" and "partly active" groups, and later by adding the "partly active" and "active" groups. Tetrachoric correlation coefficients were estimated by the method of Jenkins [4] and yielded reliability coefficients of .93 in both cases. This means that the animals are highly consistent in their behavior at this age, and that the observer was consistent in separating both the "quiet" and "active" groups from those labelled "partly active." On the other hand, the coefficient of reliability is much lower when the ratings at 5 and 6 weeks are compared, a fact which will be discussed in detail later.

When the general features of the test situation are analyzed it is found that from the viewpoint of social behavior we are dealing with a social interaction between an adult human being and an immature dog. The restraining movements of the handler may be classified as a mild form of agonistic behavior, and most of the responses of the puppy (escape behavior, crouching, sitting or lying posture, playful pawing and biting) may be included in the same category. Tail wagging and some hand licking are also observed. Dominance, or the habitual control of one individual by another by force, fighting or threats, is obviously part of the situation.

From the viewpoint of adaptation [see Fuller's situational analysis, 2], directional interactions are only moderately strong or weak. Field impedance to effective reactions is set up so that only two of the possible responses, subordinate posture and playful aggressiveness, can take place, but neither of these is more than moderately difficult. The complexity of the field is not great, but it is set up in such a way that the animals have no reliable cues for cybernetic reactions, and should tend to choose responses on the basis of innate tendencies.

The animals used consisted of populations of purebred puppies taken from the Basenji, Beagle, Cocker Spaniel, and Wire-haired Terrier breeds, and included animals up to serial number 1673. The parent population of these puppies consisted of not more than 5 or 6 animals in each case and, therefore, cannot be considered an accurate random sample of the breed. This does not affect the results of the experiment, the object of which was to study and observe differences between these samples, but it does mean that it would be incorrect to generalize concerning the whole breeds from these small samples, even if the samples themselves did not indicate a great deal of overlap between breeds.

C. RESULTS

The ratings for each animal were added together for two six-week periods beginning respectively at 5 and 11 weeks and the results averaged for each breed. These are summarizd in Table 1. No sex differences were found. It will be seen that the average rating at 5 to 10 weeks was almost exactly the same for all of the breeds except for the Cocker Spaniels, which falls much lower than the rest.

At 11 to 16 weeks the situation has changed considerably. The Beagles are almost exactly the same as before,

TABLE 1

Activity ratings of puppies being taught to remain quiet on the scales. Individual scores are expressed as the sum of 6 successive ratings, where 1 = Quiet, 2 = Partly Active, and 3 = Active. The scale used in the table therefore runs from 6 to 18

Population	n	MEAN 5-10 weeks	MEAN 11-16 weeks	SD 5-10 weeks	SD 11-16 weeks
Basenji	28	12.61 ± .4	11.04 ± .6	2.3 ± .3	3.2 ± .4
Beagle	36	12.61 ± .5	12.64 ± .7	2.7 ± .3	3.9 ± .5
Cocker Spaniel	44	9.82 ± .3	7.48 ± .2	2.2 ± .2	1.7 ± .2
Wire-haired Terrier	26	12.62 ± .6	14.65 ± .7	3.1 ± .4	3.3 ± .5
Total	134	11.59 ± .2	11.00 ± .4	2.9 ± .2	4.1 ± .2

the Basenji have fallen slightly in their activity, the Cocker Spaniels are even lower, and the Wire-haired Terriers have risen considerably. At 5-10 weeks three out of six interbreed comparisons are statistically significant, but at 11-16 weeks the number has risen to five.

The amount of variability is also interesting. At 5-10 weeks there are no significant differences except between

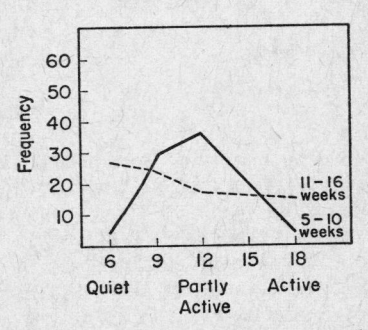

Fig. 2. Distribution of scores of the combined breed populations. Note the greatly increased individual variability at 11-16 weeks, as compared with the earlier period.

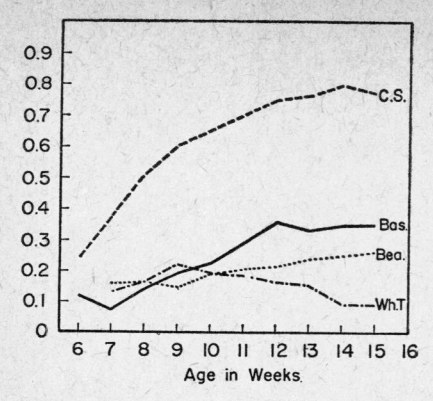

Fig. 3. Curves showing the proportion of animals rated as "quiet" in the various breed populations. The curves have been smoothed by taking the average of each three successive points. Note that there is a tendency for the values to spread out further apart as the animals grow older.

the extremes represented by the Cocker Spaniels and Basenjis on the low side and the Wire-haired Terriers on the high side. At 11-16 weeks variability has generally increased, most greatly in the animals which are nearest the middle of the distribution, and has gone down only in the Cocker Spaniels. The over-all picture (see Figure 2) shows a large increase in variability of the combined populations which may be considered as an effect of magnification of differences by habit formation.

The consistency of the behavior of individuals shows corresponding changes, as seen in Table 2. The measure used is the percentage of duplicated ratings, which is more accurate than using a tetrachoric correlation coefficient as the latter can be used only if the categories are reduced to two. (However, for purposes of rough comparison, the figure of 70 per cent in these data approximately corresponds to a tetrachoric r of .86 and a reliability coefficient of .93).

It will be seen that the results within every breed population and also for the total show an increase in

TABLE 2

Consistency of behavior, as indicated by the percentage of duplicated ratings at various ages

Breed population	5-6	AGE IN WEEKS 15-16	5-16
Basenji	46	64	29
Beagle	62	70	51
Cocker Spaniel	55	69	33
Wire-haired Terrier	50	70	40
Total	54	69	39

the consistency score when consecutive ratings at the beginning and end of the test period are compared. The Beagles appear to be different from the rest in that they show the least improvement of consistency between consecutive ratings and the greatest consistency between the early and late ratings. If training and habit formation is the essential factor involved, it would appear that the Beagles are either little affected by training, or are affected very rapidly. In any case, there is little change in this group from first till last.

This impression is borne out when the data are studied in more detail from the point of view of development. The graphs in Figures 2 and 3 show the percentage of animals which have crossed either threshold. In the case of the Cocker Spaniels the percentage of animals rated as quiet rises very steadily at a rate which is approximately 10 per cent of the animals which have not previously crossed the threshold, and the curve appears to be approaching 100 per cent as an asymptote. The same sort of thing is apparently occurring in the Basenjis at a slower rate and it does not appear that the asymptote will be much more than 70 per cent. In the Beagles the rise is very small indeed, and in the Wire-haired Terriers it may even fall slightly.

We may now consider the animals which cross the other threshold toward the active side. Among the Cocker Spaniels this proportion starts out very low and falls off to 0. In the Basenjis it rises to a peak at eight weeks of age, falling off sharply at nine weeks and then rising slightly. In the Beagles there is a very slight rise. In the Wire-haired Terriers there is a steady and fairly rapid rise which might in time reach close to 100 per cent.

A more accurate estimate of these asymptotes might be achieved by fitting curves to the data, but since the last observations are near the points where the asymptotes should be reached, a more conservative estimate of the differences can be achieved by taking the percentage of animals falling above and below each threshold during the last four trials (see Table 3).

When all possible comparisons are made between the populations in the quiet column, all but one, that between Basenjis and Beagles, are found to be significantly different from the rest. In the active column all but two of the comparisons (Basenji with Beagle and Beagle with Wire-haired Terrier) are significantly different. This compares very well with the results in Table 1 which showed that at 11 to 16 weeks all comparisons were significantly different except those between the Basenjis and Beagles.

TABLE 3

Average percentage of animals crossing either threshold, based on scores at 13-16 weeks

Breed population	% Quiet	% Active
Basenji	35	20
Beagle	26	35
Cocker Spaniel	77	0
Wire-haired Terrier	11	56

D. DISCUSSION

The data present good evidence that genetic differences affecting this particular measurement do exist and that these differences tend to increase in time under the conditions given. Of the six possible comparisons between

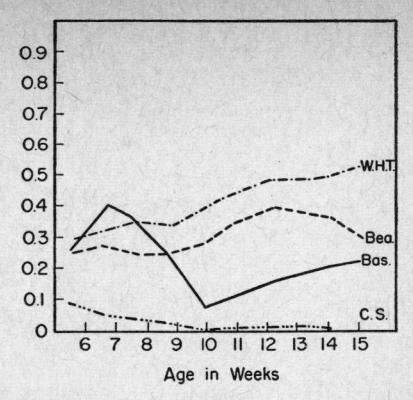

Fig. 4. Smoothed curves for the proportion of animals rated as "active" in the 4 breed populations. Again note the tendency for differences to increase. For explanation of the irregularities in the Basenji curves, see text.

breeds only one does not show significant differences at the end of the test period.

It is also clear that the case involves two separate phenomena which tend to increase the importance of genetic differences. The first of these is the magnification of differences near a threshold, which is illustrated graphically in Figure 5. Assuming that all the breed populations have the same normal distribution of genetic differences, a very good fit to their distribution into three categories (data in Table 3) can be obtained by placing the two threshold one σ apart. It will be noted that above Threshold 2 animals may be three σ apart without showing differences, but that near the threshold a difference of slightly more than one σ produces an absolute difference between "Quiet" and "Active." The figure also brings out the very considerable degree of overlap between the breed populations.

The second phenomenon is the fixation of genetic tendencies in behavior by habit formation, which tends to render behavior more consistent, and hence to magnify any original differences. This is well illustrated in Figures

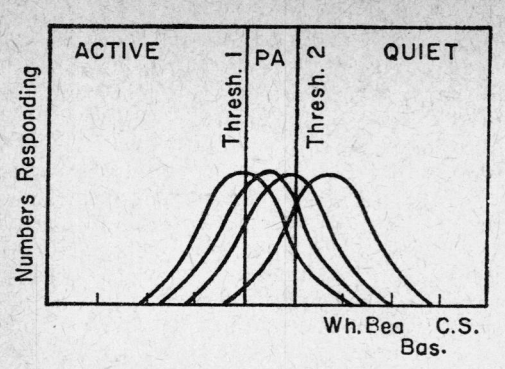

[Figure: Normalized distribution curves labeled ACTIVE, PA, QUIET with Thresh. 1 and Thresh. 2, x-axis labeled "Wh. Bas. Bea. C.S.", y-axis "Numbers Responding"]

Type of Response, σ Scale

Fig. 5. Normalized distribution of the breed populations at 11-16 weeks of age, illustrating the magnifying effects of thresholds. Assuming that all populations have the same normal distribution, a very good fit to the data can be obtained by placing the thresholds one σ apart. To the right of Threshold 2 animals may be almost three σ apart without showing differences, whereas in the middle of the scale a difference of slightly greater than one σ produces an absolute difference between "quiet" and "active." The figure also illustrates the considerable degree of overlap between the populations.

3 and 4. Animals in the "Partly Active" category show inconsistent behavior, and the proportion of animals so classified tends to decrease with time. Likewise the consistency of behavior from one trial to the next tends to increase with time. The Beagles show more original consistency and less change than the rest.

The point may be raised as to whether the increase in consistency observed is the result of training or the result of a simple maturation process. We have no control population which would test this point but other evidence would indicate that we are working with an effect of training. It has been shown that dogs are capable of habit formation at this age. During the time in which they are tested they undergo extensive handling during the other parts of the test program. Finally it has been found that animals which have been allowed to more or less run wild up to the age of 12 weeks tend to show the same or increasing amounts of escape behavior, in contrast to the increasing tameness of animals raised in the usual program.

If it may be assumed that we are correct in naming training as one of the essential factors involved we may conclude that we have an interesting case where an initial genetic difference is magnified by a threshold, and training and habit formation interact with it to still further magnify the original differences.

It should not be assumed that we are dealing with a simple unitary trait of activity or response to inhibitory training. For example, the Wire-haired Terriers, which tend to be very active while being restrained on the scales, are able to be quiet in most cases when restrained in a small cage.

From observation of this and of other tests it would appear that the behavior involved is social in nature and may be classified as agonistic, as implied in earlier paragraphs. In order that the scales may not be disturbed the handler has to touch the dogs quite gently, resulting in behavior which is apparently ambiguous as far as the puppies are concerned. The gentle restraint can be responded to as an attempt at enforcing dominance (which is the intention of the handler) or as an invitation toward playful fighting behavior. An attempt toward dominance can be responded to in at least three ways: assuming a subordinate attitude of crouching, attempting to escape, and by aggressiveness. Restraint is given in such a way that escape behavior is never effective (the puppies are never allowed to leave the scales), but the other two reactions are possible.

The Cocker Spaniels, as shown in other tests, have a strong tendency to crouch and remain still in response to human handling and this probably accounts for their quietness on the scales. The Basenjis in early life show a tendency toward escape behavior when handled but this disappears rapidly as they get older. This probably accounts for the peak in the activity rating seen in the early tests on the Basenjis. The Fox Terriers on the other hand show two tendencies, to respond with escape behavior early in life (though not as strongly as Basenjis) and later on to respond with more and more aggressive behavior. Finally, the Beagles do not show any of these traits very strongly.

It is obvious that the tendency to escape will interfere with the tendencies to be subordinate or aggressive but there is no indication as yet that any of these traits form the opposite ends of one or more scales. Rather, they appear to be alternate ways of adjusting to a situation.

James [3] has studied the reaction of a mixed population of dogs to restraint on the conditioned reflex stand. The situation is similar to the one employed in our tests except that the restraint was mechanical. He found that there were two extreme types of dogs, one which tended to become more quiet as the experiments went on day after day, eventually not reacting at all, and another which tended to become more excitable under training. Maturation as a factor which might affect consistency is ruled out in this case, since all the animals were adults. All grades of intermediate performance exist, and animals showing these are more useful for experimental purposes. No definite conclusions regarding the heredity of these traits could be drawn, but there appeared to be a tendency for certain types of behavior to be common in certain breeds.

Fuller [1] has since graded the initial response of dogs when placed on a restraining stand similar to that of James. He uses five grades from hypo- to hyperactive, and gives ratings under eight different conditions of stimulation. Presumably, if the animals were repeatedly given this treatment, results similar to those of James would be obtained. No data are yet available on breed differences.

Ratings given by Fuller in three of these situations were compared with the ratings of activity on the scales at 5-10 and 11-16 weeks [5], and almost no correlation found between them. It may be tentatively concluded that restraint by a person produces an entirely different result from restraint by mechanical means. Furthermore, neither activity on the scales nor on the stand was significantly correlated with activity in a cage.

It may be concluded that the behavior differences studied here are quite specific in nature and are not brought out in any other way except possibly by human handling in related situation.

On the other hand, both this and the results of James' experiments point to the possible existence of an important generalization which has some interesting implications. It would appear that in the higher animals genetic differences do not throw a strait jacket around the behavior of an individual. Rather, each species seems to have several ways of adjusting to a given situation. Genetic differences do not ordinarily eliminate any of these responses but affect their frequency, so that a naive animal may try out one solution to a problem more often than another. He can still give different responses when required, maintaining considerable initial flexibility of behavior, and it is only under certain conditions that genetic tendencies may result in consistent habits. However, the generality of this phenomenon must still be established.

SUMMARY

1. The ways in which small hereditary differences in behavior may be magnified by special situations are discussed theoretically.

2. When puppies are trained to stand quietly while being weighed, hereditary differences are apparently magnified in two ways: different thresholds of response to minimal repressive stimulation tend to produce all-or-none responses, and the process of habit formation tends to cause individuals to react consistently one way or the other, producing increasingly clear-cut differences.

3. The test situation is a social one involving dominance of the handler over the puppies. From the viewpoint of adaptation, and using the terms of Fuller's situational analysis, directive (motivation) factors are weak, effective interactions are simple, and no reliable cues are available for cybernetic interactions, so that the animals tend to choose responses on the basis of innate tendencies.

4. The test consists of rating puppies as "active," "partly active," or "quiet," as they stand for one minute

on the scales. Ratings are taken weekly from 5-16 weeks of age. A test of observer reliability gives a coefficient of reliability of .96, while a test of consistency between consecutive tests gives a figure of .93 at 15-16 weeks of age.

5. The populations tested consist of 28 Basenjis, 36 Beagles, 44 Cocker Spaniels, and 26 Wire-haired Terriers.

6. When analyzed, the results show that the Cocker Spaniels are at first significantly different from the other three populations and tend to become increasingly quiet, finally reaching a figure of 77 per cent quiet and 0 per cent active.

7. The Beagle population shows little change, either in average ratings or consistency, indicating that the animals are little affected by training of the sort given during the period of 5-16 weeks of age.

8. The majority of the Wire-haired Terriers become increasingly active, finally reaching a figure of 56 per cent active and 11 per cent quiet.

9. The Basenjis show approximately equal numbers of animals which tend to become quiet and active (final figures 35 and 20 per cent).

10. The effect on the total population is one of greatly increased variability from early to later tests, which may be interpreted as the result of habit formation increasing consistency and thus magnifying genetic variability.

11. Relevant data from other sources are discussed, and it is concluded that a tentative generalization may be drawn; namely, that hereditary differences in behavior of the higher animals tend to cause an individual to choose one of several alternate modes of behavior with greater frequency than others, this tendency becoming consistent with habit formation under certain situations. Thus, identically treated animals may show smaller and less consistent differences before than after training.

REFERENCES

1. FULLER, J. L., Individual differences in the reactivity of dogs. *J. Comp. & Phys. Psychol.*, 1948, 41, 339-347.

2. ———, Situational analysis; a classification of organism-field reactions. *Psychol. Rev.*, 1950, 57, 3-18.
3. JAMES, W. T., Morphological form and its relation to behavior. In: STOCKARD, C. R., *The genetic and endocrine basis for differences in form and behavior*. Phila.: Wistar Institute, 1941.
4. JENKINS, W. L., A single chart for tetrachoric *r*. *Educ. & Psychol. Meas.*, 1950, 10, 142-144.
5. ROYCE, J. R., A factorial analysis of emotionality in the dog. Chicago: Univ. Chicago (Ph.D. Thesis (MS)), 1951.
6. SCOTT, J. P., Effects of single genes on the behavior of Drosophila. *Am. Nat.*, 1943, 77, 184-190.
7. ———, The magnification of differences by a threshold. *Science*, 1944, 100, 569-570.
8. ———, Incomplete adjustment caused by frustration of untrained fighting mice. *J. Comp. Psychol.*, 1946, 39, 379-390.
9. SCOTT, J. P., AND CHARLES, M. S., Some problems of heredity and social behavior. *J. Gen. Psychol.* (In Press.)
10. SCOTT, J. P., AND FULLER, J. L. (Eds.), *A manual of dog-testing techniques* (mimeographed). Bar Harbor: R. B. Jackson Memorial Laboratory, 1950.
11. SCOTT, J. P., AND FULLER, J. L., Research on genetics and social behavior at the Roscoe B. Jackson Memorial Laboratory, 1946-1951—a progress report. *J. Hered.*, 1951, 42, 191-197.

13

Problems Raised by Instinct Theories

DANIEL S. LEHRMAN

This article originally appeared in the *Quarterly Review of Biology*, 1953, Vol. 28, pp. 337-365 (excerpted).

Even this brief summary brings to light several questions which ought to be critically examined with reference to the theory. These are questions, furthermore, which apply to instinct theories in general. Among them are: (1) the problem of "innateness" and the maturation of behavior; (2) the problem of levels of organization in an organism; (3) the nature of evolutionary levels of behavioral organization, and the use of the comparative method in studying them; and (4) the manner in which physiological concepts may be properly used in behavior analysis. There follows an evaluation of Lorenz's theory in terms of these general problems.

"INNATENESS" OF BEHAVIOR

The Problem

Lorenz and Tinbergen consistently speak of behavior as being "innate" or "inherited" as though these words surely referred to a definable, definite, and delimited category of behavior. It would be impossible to overestimate the heuristic value which they imply for the concepts "innate" and "not-innate." Perhaps the most effective way to throw light on the "instinct" problem is to consider carefully just what it means to say that a mode of behavior is innate, and how much insight this kind of statement gives into the origin and nature of the behavior.

Tinbergen (1942), closely following Lorenz, speaks of instinctive acts as "highly stereotyped, coordinated movements, the neuromotor apparatus of which belongs, in its complete form, to the hereditary constitution of the animal." Lorenz (1939) speaks of characteristics of behavior which are "hereditary, individually fixed, and thus open to evolutionary analysis." Lorenz (1935) also refers to perceptual patterns ("releasers") which are presumed to be innate because they elicit "instinctive" behavior the *first time* they are presented to the animal. He also refers to those motor patterns as innate which occur for the first time when the proper stimuli are presented. Lorenz's student Grohmann (1938), as well as Tinbergen and Kuenen (1939), speak of behavior as being innately determined because it matures instead of developing through learning.

It is thus apparent that Lorenz and Tinbergen, by "innate" behavior, mean behavior which is hereditarily determined, which is part of the original constitution of the animal, which arises quite independently of the animal's experience and environment, and which is distinct from acquired or learned behavior.

It is also apparent, explicitly or implicitly, that Lorenz and Tinbergen regard as the major criteria of innateness that: (1) the behavior be stereotyped and constant in form, (2) it be characteristic of the species; (3) it appear in animals which have been raised in isolation from others; and (4) it develop fully-formed in animals which have been prevented from practicing it.

Undoubtedly, there are behavior patterns which meet these criteria. Even so, this does not necessarily imply that Lorenz's *interpretation* of these behavior patterns as "innate" offers genuine aid to a scientific understanding of their origin and of the mechanisms underlying them.

In order to examine the soundness of the concept of "innateness" in the analysis of behavior, it will be instructive to start with a consideration of one or two behavior patterns which have already been analyzed to some extent.

Pecking in the Chick

Domestic chicks characteristically begin to peck at objects, including food grains, soon after hatching (Shepard and Breed, 1913; Bird, 1925; Cruze, 1935; and others). The pecking behavior consists of at least three highly stereotyped components: head lunging, bill opening and closing, and swallowing. They are ordinarily coordinated into a single resultant act of lunging at the grain while opening the bill, followed by swallowing when the grain is picked up. This coordination is present to some extent soon after hatching, and improves later (even, to a slight extent, if the chick is prevented from practicing).

This pecking is stereotyped, characteristic of the species, appears in isolated chicks, is present at the time of hatching, and shows some improvement in the absence of specific practice. Obviously, it qualifies as an "innate" behavior, in the sense used by Lorenz and Tinbergen.

Kuo (1932a-d) has studied the embryonic development of the chick in a way which throws considerable light on the origin of this "innate" behavior. As early as three days of embryonic age, the neck is passively bent when the heartbeat causes the head (which rests on the thorax) to rise and fall. The head is stimulated tactually by the yolk sac, which is moved mechanically by amnion contractions synchronized with the heartbeats which cause head movement. Beginning about one day later, the head first bends *actively* in response to tactual stimulation. At about this time, too, the bill begins to open and close when the bird nods—according to Kuo, apparently through nervous excitation furnished by the head movements through irradiation in the still-incomplete nervous system. Bill-opening and closing become independent of head-activity only somewhat later. After about 8 or 9 days, fluid forced into the throat by the bill and head movements causes swallowing. On the twelfth day, bill-opening always follows head-movement.

In the light of Kuo's studies the "innateness" of the chick's pecking takes on a different character from that suggested by the concept of a unitary, innate item of behavior. Kuo's observations strongly suggest several interpretations of the *development* of pecking (which, of course, are subject to further clarification). For example, the head-lunge arises from the passive head-bending which occurs contiguously with tactual stimulation of the head while the nervous control of the muscles is being established. By the time of hatching, head-lunging in response to tactual stimulation is very well established (in fact, it plays a major role in the hatching process).

The genesis of head-lunging to visual stimulation in the chick has not been analyzed. In Amblystoma, however, Coghill (1929) has shown that a closely analogous shift from tactual to visual control is a consequence of the establishment of certain anatomical relationships between the optic nerve and the brain region which earlier mediated the lunging response to tactual stimulation, so that visual stimuli come to elicit responses established during a period of purely tactual sensitivity. If a similar situation obtains in the chick, we would be dealing with a case of intersensory equivalence, in which visual stimuli, because of the anatomical relationships between the visual and tactual regions of the brain, became equivalent to tactual stimuli, which in turn became effective through an already analyzed process of development, which involved conditioning at a very early age (Maier and Schneirla, 1935).

The originally diffuse connection between head-lunge and bill-opening appears to be strengthened by the repeated elicitation of lunging and billing by tactual stimulation by the yolk sac. The repeated elicitation of swallowing by the pressure of amniotic fluid following bill-opening probably is important in the establishment of the post-hatching integration of bill-opening and swallowing.

Maternal Behavior in the Rat

Another example of behavior appearing to fulfil the criteria of "innateness" may be found in the maternal behavior of the rat.

Pregnant female rats build nests by piling up strips of paper or other material. Mother rats will "retrieve" their pups to the nest by picking them up in the mouth and carrying them back to the nest. Nest-building and retrieving both occur in all normal rats; they occur in rats which have been raised in isolation; and they occur with no evidence of previous practice, since both are performed well by primiparous rats (retrieving may take place for the first time only a few minutes after the birth of the first litter of a rat raised in isolation). Both behavior patterns therefore appear to satisfy the criteria of "innateness" (Wiesner and Sheard, 1933).

Reiss (pers. com.), however, raised rats in isolation, at the same time preventing them from ever manipulating or carrying any objects. The floor of the living cage was of netting so that feces dropped down out of reach. All food was powdered, so that the rats never carried food pellets. When mature, these rats were placed in regular breeding cages. They bred, but did *not* build normal nests or retrieve their young normally. They scattered nesting material all over the floor of the cage, and similarly moved the young from place to place without collecting them at a nest-place.

Female rats do a great deal of licking of their own genitalia, particularly during pregnancy (Wiesner and Sheard, 1933). This increased licking during pregnancy has several probable bases, the relative importance of which is not yet known. The increased need of the pregnant rat for potassium salts (Heppel and Schmidt, 1938) probably accounts in part for the increased licking of the salty body fluids as does the increased irritability of the genital organs themselves. Birch (pers. com.) has suggested that this genital licking may play an important role in the development of licking and retrieving of the young. He is raising female rats fitted from an early age with collars made of rubber discs, so worn that the rat is effectively prevented from licking its genitalia. Present indications, based on limited data, are that rats so raised eat a high percentage of their young, that the young in the nest may be found under any part of the female instead of concentrated posteriorly as with normal mother rats, and that retrieving does not occur.

These considerations raise some questions concerning

nativistic interpretations of nest-building and retrieving in the rat, and concerning the meaning of the criteria of "innateness." To begin with, it is apparent that practice in carrying food pellets is partly equivalent, for the development of nest-building and retrieving, to practice in carrying nesting-material, and in carrying the young. Kinder (1927) has shown that nest-building activity is inversely correlated with environmental temperature, and that it can be stopped by raising the temperature sufficiently. This finding, together with Riess's experiment, suggests that the nest-building activity arises from ordinary food (and other object) manipulation and collection under conditions where the accumulation of certain types of manipulated material leads to immediate satisfaction of one of the animal's needs (warmth). The fact that the rat is generally more active at lower temperatures (Browman, 1943: Morgan, 1947) also contributes to the probability that nest-building activity will develop. In addition, the rat normally tends to stay close to the walls of its cage, and thus to spend much time in corners. This facilitates the collection of nesting material into one corner of the cage, and the later retrieving of the young to that corner. Patrick and Laughlin (1934) has shown that rats raised in an environment without opaque walls do not develop this "universal" tendency of rats to walk close to the wall. Birch's experiment suggests that the rat's experience in licking its own genitalia helps to establish retrieving as a response to the young, as does its experience in carrying food and nesting material.

Maturation-vs.-Learning, Or Development?
The Isolation Experiment

These studies suggest some second thoughts on the nature of the "isolation experiment." It is obvious that by the criteria used by Lorenz and other instinct theorists, pecking in the chick and nest-building and retrieving in the rat are not "learned" behavior. They fulfill all criteria of "innateness," i.e., of behavior which develops without opportunity for practice or imitation. Yet, in each case, analysis of the developmental process involved shows that the behavior patterns concerned are not unitary, autonomously developing things, but rather that they emerge ontogenetically in complex ways from the previously developed organization of the organism in a given setting.

What, then, is wrong with the implication of the "isolation experiment," that behavior developed in isolation may be considered "innate" if the animal did not practice it specifically?

Lorenz repeatedly refers to behavior as being innate because it is displayed by animals raised in isolation. The raising of rats in isolation, and their subsequent testing for nesting behavior, is typical of isolation experiments. The development of the chick inside the egg might be regarded as the ideal isolation experiment.

It must be realized that an animal raised in isolation from fellow-members of his species *is not necessarily isolated from the effect of processes and events which contribute to the development of any particular behavior pattern*. The important question is not "Is the animal isolated?" but *"From what is the animal isolated?"* The isolation experiment, if the conditions are well analyzed, provides at best a negative indication that certain specified environmental factors probably are not directly involved in the genesis of a particular behavior. However, the isolation experiment by its very nature does not give a positive indication that behavior is "innate" or indeed any information at all about what the process of development of the behavior really consisted of. The example of the nest-building and retrieving by rats which are isolated from other rats but not from their food pellets or from their own genitalia illustrates the danger of assuming "innateness" merely because a *particular* hypothesis about learning seems to be disproved. This is what is consistently done by Tinbergen, as, for example, when he says (1942) of certain behavior patterns of the three-spined stickleback: "The releasing mechanisms of these reactions are all innate. A male that was reared in isolation . . . was tested with models before it had ever seen another stickleback. The . . . (stimuli) . . . had the same releaser functions as in the experiments with normal males." Such isolation is by no means a final or complete control on possible effects from experience. For example, is the "isolated" fish uninfluenced by its own reflection from a water film or glass wall? Is the animal's experience with human handlers, food objects, etc., really irrelevant?

Similarly, Howells and Vine (1940) have reported that chicks raised in mixed flocks of two varieties, when tested in a Y-maze, learn to go to chicks of their own variety more readily than to those of the other variety. They concluded that the "learning is accelerated or retarded . . . because of the directive influence of innate factors." In this case, Schneirla (1946) suggests that the effect of the chick's experience with its own chirping during feeding has not been adequately considered as a source of differential learning previous to the experiment. This criticism may also be made of a similar study by Schoolland (1942) using chicks and ducklings.

Even more fundamental is the question of what is meant by "maturation." We may ask whether experiments based on the assumption of an absolute dichotomy between maturation and learning ever really tell us *what* is maturing, or how it is maturing? When the question is examined in terms of *developmental* processes and relationships, rather than in terms of preconceived categories, the maturation-versus-learning formulation of the problem is more or less dissipated. For example, in the rat nest-building probably does not mature autonomously —and it is *not* learned. It is *not* "nest-building" which is learned. Nest-building develops in certain situations through a developmental process in which at each stage there is an identifiable interaction between the environment and organic processes, and within the organism, this interaction is based on the preceding stage of development and gives rise to the succeeding stage. These interactions are present from the earliest (zygote) stage. Learning may emerge as a factor in the animal's behavior even at early embryonic stages, as pointed out by Carmichael (1936).

Pecking in the chick is also an emergent—an integration of head, bill, and throat components, each of which has its own developmental history. This integration is already partially established by the time of hatching, providing a clear example of "innate" behavior in which the statement "it is innate" adds nothing to an understanding of the development process involved. The statement that "pecking" is innate, or that it "matures," leads us *away* from any attempt to analyze its specific origins. The assumption that pecking grows *as* a pecking *pattern* discourages examination of the embryological processes leading to pecking. The elements out of whose interaction pecking emerges are not originally a unitary pattern; they *become* related as a consequence of their positions in the organization of the embryonic chick. The understanding provided by Kuo's observations owes nothing to the "maturation-versus-learning" formulation.

Observations such as these suggest many new problems the relevance of which is not apparent when the patterns are nativistically interpreted. For example, what is the nature of the rat's temperature-sensitivity which enables its nest-building to vary with temperature? How does the animal develop its ability to handle food in specific ways? What are the physiological conditions which promote licking of the genitalia, etc.? We want to know much more about the course of establishment of the connections between the chick's head-lunge and bill-opening, and between bill-opening and swallowing. This does *not* mean that we expect to establish which of the components is learned and which matured, or "how much" each is learned and how much matured. The effects of learning and of structural factors differ, not only from component to component of the pattern, but also from developmental stage to developmental stage. What is required is a continuation of the careful analysis of the characteristics of each developmental stage, and of the transition from each stage to the next.

Our scepticism regarding the heuristic value of the concept of "maturation" should not be interpreted as ignorance or denial of the fact that the physical growth of varied structures plays an important role in the development of most of the kinds of behavior patterns under discussion in the present paper. Our objection is to the *interpretation* of the role of this growth that is implied in the notion that the *behavior* (or a *specific* physiological substrate for it) is "maturing." For example, the post-hatching improvement in pecking ability of chicks is very probably due in part to an increase in strength of the leg muscles and to an increase in balance and stability of the standing chick, which results partly from this strengthening of the legs and partly from the development of equilibrium responses (Cruze, 1935). Now, isolation or prevention-of-practice experiments would lead to the conclusion that this part of the improvement was due to "maturation." Of course it is partly due to growth processes, *but what is growing is not pecking ability*, just as, when the skin temperature receptors of the rat develop, what is growing is not nest-building activity, *or anything isomorphic with it*. The use of the categories "maturation-vs.-learning" as explanatory aids usually gives a false impression of unity and directedness in the growth of the behavior pattern, when actually the behavior pattern is not primarily unitary, nor does development proceed in a straight line toward the completion of the pattern.

It is apparent that the use of the concept of "maturation" by Lorenz and Tinbergen as well as by many other workers is not, as it at first appears, a reference to a process of development but rather to ignoring the process of development. To say of a behavior that it develops by maturation is tantamount to saying that the obvious forms of learning do not influence it, and that we therefore do not consider it necessary to investigate its ontogeny further.

Heredity-vs.-Environment, or Development?

Much the same kind of problem arises when we consider the question of what is "inherited." It is characteristic of Lorenz, as of instinct theorists in general, that "instinctive acts" are regarded by him as "inherited." Furthermore, inherited behavior is regarded as sharply distinct from behavior acquired through "experience." Lorenz (1937a) refers to behavior which develops "entirely independent of all experience."

It has become customary, in recent discussions of the "heredity-environment" problem, to state that the "hereditary" and "environmental" contributions are both essential to the development of the organism; that the organism could not develop in the absence of either, and that the dichotomy is more or less artificial. (This formulation, however, frequently serves as an introduction to elaborate attempts to evaluate what part, or even what percentage, of behavior is genetically determined and what part acquired (Howells, 1945; Beach, 1947a; Carmichael, 1947; Stone, 1947).) Lorenz does not make even this much of a concession to the necessity of developmental analysis. He simply states that some behavior patterns are "inherited," others "acquired by individual experiences." I do not know of any statement of either Lorenz or Tinbergen which would allow the reader to conclude that they have any doubts about the correctness of referring to behavior as simply "inherited" or "genetically controlled."

Now, what exactly is meant by the statement that a behavior pattern is "inherited" or "genetically controlled"? Lorenz undoubtedly does not think that the zygote contains the instinctive act in miniature, or that the gene is the equivalent of an entelechy which purposefully and continuously tries to push the organism's development in a particular direction. Yet one or both of these preformistic assumptions, or their equivalents, must underlie the notion that some behavior patterns are "inherited" as such.

The "instinct" is obviously not present in the zygote. Just as obviously, it is present in the behavior of the animal after the appropriate age. The problem for the investigator who wishes to make a causal analysis of behavior is: How did this behavior come about? The use of "explanatory" categories such as "innate" and "genetically fixed" obscures the necessity of investigating developmental *processes* in order to gain insight into the actual mechanisms of behavior and their interrelations. The problem of development is the problem of the development of new structures and activity patterns from the resolution of the interaction of *existing* structures and patterns, within the organism and its internal environment, and between the organism and its outer environment. At any stage of development, the new features emerge from the interactions within the *current* stage and between the *current* stage and the environment. The interaction out of which the organism develops is *not* one, as is so often said, between heredity and environment. It is between *organism* and environment! And the organism is different at each different stage of its development.

Modern physiological and biochemical genetics is fast destroying the conception of a straight-line relationship between gene and somatic characteristic. For example, certain strains of mice contain a mutant gene called "dwarf." Mice homozygous for "dwarf" are smaller than normal mice. It has been shown (Smith and MacDowell, 1930; Keeler, 1931) that the cause of this dwarfism is a deficiency of pituitary growth hormone secretion. Now what are we to regard as "inherited"? Shall we change the name of the mutation from "dwarf" to "pituitary dysfunction" and say that dwarfism is not inherited as such—that what is inherited is a hypoactive pituitary gland? This would merely push the problem back to an earlier stage of development. We now have a better understanding of the origin of the dwarfism than we did when we could only say it is "genetically determined." However, the pituitary function developed, in turn, in the context of the mouse as it was when the gland was developing. The problem is "What was that context and how did the gland develop out of it?"

What, then, is inherited? From a somewhat similar argument, Jennings (1930) and Chein (1936) concluded that only the zygote is inherited, or that heredity is only a stage of development. There is no point here in involving ourselves in tautological arguments over the definition of heredity. It is clear, however, that to say a behavior pattern is "inherited" throws no light on its *development* except for the purely negative implication that certain types of learning are not directly involved. Dwarfism in the mouse, nest-building in the rat, pecking in the chick, and the "zig-zag dance" of the stickleback's courtship (Tinbergen, 1942) are all "inherited" in the sense and by the criteria used by Lorenz. But they are not by any means phenomena of a common type, nor do they arise through the same kinds of developmental processes. To lump them together under the rubric of "inherited" or "innate" characteristics serves to block the investigation of their origin just at the point where it should leap forward in meaningfulness. (Anastasi and Foley (1948), considering data from the field of human differential psychology have been led to somewhat the same formulation of the "heredity-environment" problem as is presented here.)

14

The Descent of Instinct

FRANK A. BEACH

This article originally appeared in the *Psychology Review*, 1955, Vol. 62, pp. 401-410.

"The delusion is extraordinary by which we thus exalt language above nature: making language the expositor of nature, instead of making nature the expositor of language" (Alexander Brian Johnson, *A Treatise on Language*).

The basic ideas underlying a concept of instinct probably are older than recorded history. At any rate they are clearly set forth in the Greek literature of 2,500 years ago. They have been controversial ideas and they remain so today. Nevertheless, the instinct concept has survived in almost complete absence of empirical validation. One aim of the present article is to analyze the reasons for the remarkable vitality of a concept which has stood without objective test for at least two millennia. A second objective is to evaluate the concept as it relates to a science of behavior.

ORIGINS IN PHILOSOPHY AND THEOLOGY

The concept of instinct evolved in relation to the broad problems of human destiny, of Man's place in nature, and his position in this world and the next. From the beginning, instinct has been defined and discussed in terms of its relation to reason and, less directly, to the human soul.

During the fourth century B.C., the Greek philosopher Heraclitus declared that there had been two types of creation. Men and gods were the products of rational creation, whereas irrational brutes comprised a separate category of living creatures. Heraclitus added the observation that only gods and men possess souls. The close relation between rational powers and possession of a soul has been reaffirmed time and again during the ensuing 2,500 years. Heraclitus did not advance the concept of instinct but he laid the groundwork for its development.

Stoic philosophers of the first century A.D. held that men and gods belong to one natural community, since they are rational beings. All animals were specifically excluded since they are not creatures of reason and even their most complex behavior takes place "without reflection," to use the words of Seneca. This stoical taxonomy was both flattering and convenient since, according to the tenets of this school, members of the natural community were forbidden to harm or enslave other members.

It is significant that neither Heraclitus nor the Stoics based their conclusions upon objective evidence. Their premises concerning the psychology of animals were not derived from empirical observation; they were demanded by assumption of the philosophical position that animals lack a rational soul.

Aristotle, who was more of an observer than a philosopher, was of a different mind. In 'Historia Animalium' Man is placed at the top of Scala Natura (directly above the Indian elephant), and is accorded superior intellectual powers, but none qualitatively distinct from those of other species.

In the thirteenth century Albertus Magnus composed 'De Animalibus,' based chiefly upon the writings of Aristotle but modifying the Aristotelian position where necessary to conform to Scholastic theology. Albertus removed Man from the natural scale, holding that he is unique in possessing the gift of reason and an immortal soul. Animals, lacking reason, "are directed by their natural instinct and therefore cannot act freely."

St. Thomas Aquinas, student of Albertus, supported his teacher's distinction between men and animals.

Animals possess only the sensitive soul described by Aristotle. The human embryo is similarly endowed, but the rational soul is divinely implanted in the fetus at some time before birth.* The behavior of man therefore depends upon reason, whereas all animals are governed by instinct. Like the Stoic philosophers, the Scholastics were unconcerned with factual evidence. Their emphasis upon instinctive control of animal behavior was dictated by a need of the theological system, and in this frame of reference instinct was a useful concept.

Roughly four centuries after the time of St. Thomas Aquinas, René Descartes and his followers aggressively restated the existence of a man-brute dichotomy. The bare facts of the Cartesian position are common knowledge, but for the purpose of the present argument it is important to ask why Descartes felt so strongly about the matter—felt compelled to hold up man as the Reasoner, at the same time insisting that all other living creatures are only flesh-and-blood machines. The explanation stands out in the following quotation:

"After the error of atheism, there is nothing that leads weak minds further astray from the paths of virtue than the idea that the minds of other animals resemble our own, and that therefore we have no greater right to future life than have gnats and ants." (René Descartes, 'Passions of the Soul'.)

From Albertus to Descartes the argument runs clear. The theological system posits a life after death. Hence the postulation of the soul. But mere possession of a soul is not enough. Each man must earn the right of his soul's salvation. This in turn depends upon reason, which man exercises in differentiating good from evil, behavior which is sinful from that which is not. An afterlife is man's unique prerogative; no animals share it. They have no souls and therefore no need to reason. But how are the complex and adaptive reactions of subhuman creatures to be explained if not by reason, foresight, volition?

* It is not irrelevant to point out that weighty disputation concerning the exact age at which the soul enters the fetus retarded the advancement of embryological knowledge during its 17th century beginnings.

They are comfortably disposed of as products of instincts with which the Creator has endowed all dumb brutes.

That the thirteenth-century point of view persists today is shown by the following quotation:

"In animals there are only instincts, but not in man. As St. Thomas points out, there cannot be any deliberation in a subrational being (even though we may get the impression that there is). . . . Instincts in animals seem to operate according to the pattern of physical forces, where the stronger always prevails; for animals are utterly devoid of the freedom which characterizes man. . . . That is why when one studies human behavior one must rise above the purely animal pattern and concentrate upon those two faculties, intellect and will, which separate man from animal." (Msgr. Fulton J. Sheen, 'Peace of Soul.')

To summarize what has been said thus far, it appears that the descent of the instinct concept can be traced from early philosophies which set man apart from the rest of the living world and sought for him some divine affinity. This was achieved by claiming for man alone the power of reason. By a process of elimination the behavior of animals was ascribed to their natural instincts. During the Middle Ages this dichotomous classification became a part of Church doctrine, with the result that possession of reason and of a soul were inextricably linked to the hope of eternal life. Prescientific concepts of instinct were not deduced from the facts of nature; they were necessitated by the demands of philosophical systems based upon supernatural conceptions of nature.

EARLY SCIENTIFIC USAGE

When biology emerged as a scientific discipline, there was a general tendency to adopt the prescientific point of view regarding instinct. Some exceptions occurred. For example, Erasmus Darwin's 'Zoonomia' expressed the theory that all behavior is a product of experience, but this point of view was subsequently disavowed by the grandson of its sponsor. Charles Darwin made the concept of instinct one cornerstone of his theory of evolution by means of natural selection.

To bridge the gap of the Cartesian man-brute dichotomy, and thus to establish the evolution of mind as well as structure, Darwin and his disciples amassed two types of evidence. One type purported to prove the existence of human instincts, the other pertained to rational behavior in subhuman species. The idea of discontinuity in mental evolution was vigorously attacked, but the dichotomy between instinct and reason was never challenged.

The nineteenth-century literature on evolution shows plainly that the concept of instinctive behavior was accepted because it filled a need in the theoretical system, and not because its validity had been established by empirical test.

Contemporary psychologists such as Herbert Spencer were influenced by the evolutionary movement, and the idea of an instinctive basis for human psychology became popular. William James, in Volume II of his 'Principles,' insisted that man has more instincts than any other mammal. McDougall's widely read 'Social Psychology' listed human instincts of flight, repulsion, parental feeling, reproduction, self-abasement, etc. Woodworth, Thorndike, and other leaders agreed that much of human behavior is best understood as an expression of instinctive drives or needs.

One of the difficulties with such thinking is that it often leads to the nominal fallacy—the tendency to confuse naming with explaining. Some psychological writers were guilty of employing the instinct concept as an explanatory device, and the eventual result was a vigorous revolt against the use of instinct in any psychological theory.

THE ANTI-INSTINCT REVOLT

Dunlap's 1919 article, "Are there any instincts?" [5], was one opening gun in the battle, but the extreme protests came from the most radical Behaviorists as represented by Z. Y. Kuo, who wrote on the subject, "A psychology without heredity" [18]. For a while the word "instinct" was anathema, but the revolt was abortive, and there were three principal reasons for its failure.

First, Kuo denied instinct but admitted the existence of unlearned "units of reaction." By this phrase he meant simple reflexes, but in using it he set up a dichotomy of learned and unlearned behavior which was fatal to his basic thesis. It merely shifted the debate to arguments as to the degree of complexity permissible in an unlearned response, or the proportion of a complex pattern that was instinctive. The second error consisted essentially of a return to the position taken by Erasmus Darwin at the close of the eighteenth century. Having averred that the only unlearned reactions consist of a few simple reflexes, the opponents of the instinct doctrine invoked learning to explain all other behavior. This forced them into untenable positions such as that of maintaining that pecking behavior of the newly-hatched chick is a product of head movements made by the embryo in the shell, or that the neo-natal infant's grasp reflex depends upon prenatal exercise of this response. The third loophole in the anti-instinct argument derived from a dualistic concept of the hereditary process. Admitting that genes can affect morphological characters, and simultaneously denying that heredity influences behavior, opponents of instinct were hoist by their own petard. If the physical machinery for behavior develops under genetic control, then the behavior it mediates can scarcely be regarded as independent of inheritance.

It is important to note that this war over instinct was fought more with words and inferential reasoning than with behavioral evidence. It is true that a few individuals actually observed the behavior of newborn children or of animals, but most of the battles of the campaign were fought from the armchair in the study rather than from the laboratory.

CURRENT THOUGHT IN PSYCHOLOGY

Although there are militant opponents of the instinct doctrine among present-day psychologists, it is undoubtedly correct to say that the concept of instincts as complex, unlearned patterns of behavior is generally accepted in clinical, social, and experimental psychology. Among experimentalists, Lashley suggested that instinctive behavior is unlearned and differs from reflexes in that instincts depend on "the pattern or organization of the stimulus," whereas reflexes are elicited by stimulation of localized groups of sensory endings [19].

Carmichael [3] expressed agreement with G. H. Parker's statement that human beings are "about nine-tenths inborn, and one-tenth acquired." Morgan [20] studied food-hoarding behavior in rats, and concluded, "since it comes out spontaneously without training, it is plainly instinctive." The following quotation reveals that some modern psychologists not only embrace the concept of instinctive behavior but consider it a useful explanatory device.

"Of the theories of hoarding which have been advanced, the most reasonable one in terms of recent data is that the behavior is instinctive. . . ." [23].

At least three serious criticisms can be leveled against current treatment of the problem of instinctive behavior. The first is that psychologists in general actually know very little about most of the behavior patterns which they confidently classify as instinctive. In his paper, "The experimental analysis of instinctive activities," Lashley mentions the following 15 examples:

1. Eating of Hydra by the Planarian, Microstoma.
2. Nest-building, cleaning of young and retrieving by the primiparous rat.
3. Restless running about of the mother rat deprived of her litter.
4. Homing of pigeons.
5. Web-weaving of spiders.
6. Migratory behavior of fishes.
7. Nest-building of birds, including several species.
8. Mating behavior of the female rat in estrus.
9. Dancing reactions of the honeybee returning to the hive laden with nectar.
10. Visual reactions of rats reared in darkness.
11. Responses of the sooty tern to her nest and young.

12. Reactions of the seagull to artificial and normal eggs.
13. Sexual behavior of the male rat.
14. Mating responses in insects.
15. Mating responses in domestic hens.

It is a safe guess that most American psychologists have never observed any of these patterns of behavior. At a conservative estimate, less than half of the reactions listed have been subjected to even preliminary study by psychologically trained investigators. The significance of this criticism lies partly in the fact that those psychologists who *have* worked in the area of "instinctive" behavior tend to be more critical of the instinct concept than are those who lack first hand knowledge of the behavioral evidence.

Relevant to the criticism of unfamiliarity is the fact that the degree of assurance with which instincts are attributed to a given species is inversely related to the extent to which that species has been studied, particularly from the developmental point of view. Before the development of complex behavior in human infants had been carefully analyzed, it was, as we have seen, a common practice to describe many human instincts. Longitudinal studies of behavior have reduced the "unlearned" components to three or four simple responses not much more complex than reflexes [4].

The second criticism is that despite prevailing ignorance about the behavior which is called instinctive, there is strong pressure toward premature categorization of the as yet unanalyzed patterns of reaction. The history of biological taxonomy shows that the reliability of any classificatory system is a function of the validity of identification of individual specimens or even populations. Unless the systematist is thoroughly familiar with the characteristics of a given species, he cannot determine its proper relation to other groups. Similarly, until psychologists have carefully analyzed the salient characteristics of a given pattern of behavior, they cannot meaningfully classify or compare it with other patterns.

The third criticism of current treatment of instinctive

behavior has to do with the classificatory scheme which is in use. When all criteria which supposedly differentiate instinctive from acquired responses are critically evaluated, the only one which seems universally applicable is that instincts are unlearned [21]. This forces psychology to deal with a two-class system, and such systems are particularly unmanageable when one class is defined solely in negative terms, that is, in terms of the absence of certain characteristics that define the other class. It is logically indefensible to categorize any behavior as unlearned unless the characteristics of learned behavior have been thoroughly explored and are well known. Even the most optimistic "learning psychologist" would not claim that we have reached this point yet. At present, to prove that behavior is unlearned is equivalent to proving the null hypothesis.

Perhaps a more serious weakness in the present psychological handling of instinct lies in the assumption that a two-class system is adequate for the classification of complex behavior. The implication that all behavior must be determined by learning or by heredity, neither of which is more than partially understood, is entirely unjustified. The final form of any response is affected by a multiplicity of variables, only two of which are genetical and experiential factors. It is to the identification and analysis of all of these factors that psychology should address itself. When this task is properly conceived and executed, there will be no need nor reason for ambiguous concepts of instinctive behavior.

GENES AND BEHAVIOR

Experimental investigation of relationships between genetical constitution and behavior was exemplified by the pioneering studies of Yerkes [30], Tryon [27], and Heron [12]. Interest in this area has recently increased, and a large number of investigations have been summarized by Hall [11], who anticipates a new inter-disciplinary science of psychogenetics.

As Hall points out, the psychologist interested in examining gene-behavior relations has several approaches to choose from. He can compare the behavior of different inbred strains of animals currently available in the genetics laboratory. He can cross two strains and study the behavior of the hybrids. Selective breeding for particular behavioral traits is a well-established technique. The behavioral effects of induced mutations have as yet received very little attention but should be investigated.

It is known that selective breeding can alter the level of general activity [23], maze behavior [12], emotionality [9], and aggressiveness [17] in the laboratory rat. Inbred strains of mice differ from one another in temperature preference [13], aggressiveness [24], and strength of "exploratory drive" [26].

Various breeds of dogs exhibit pronounced differences in behavioral characteristics. Some are highly emotional, unstable and restless; whereas others are phlegmatic and relatively inactive [7]. Special breeds have been created by selective mating to meet certain practical requirements. For example, some hunting dogs such as the foxhound are "open trailers." While following a fresh trail they vocalize in a characteristic fashion. Other dogs are "mute trailers." The F_1 hybrids of a cross between these types are always open trailers although the voice is often that of the mute trailing parent [29].

Inbreeding of domestic chickens for high egg production has produced behavioral deficiencies of various kinds. Although hens of some lines are excellent layers, they have almost totally lost the normal tendency to brood the eggs once they have been laid [15]. The maternal behavior of sows of different inbred lines of swine is strikingly different. Females of one line are so aggressively protective of their young that they cannot be approached during the lactation period. Sows of a second genetical line possess such weak maternal interest that they frequently kill their litters by stepping or lying on the young [14].

Study of the effects of controlled breeding cast doubt upon the validity of any classificatory system which describes one type of behavior as genetically determined and another as experientially determined. For example, by manipulating the genotype it is possible to alter certain types of learning ability. As far as present evidence can show, the influence of genes on learning is as important as any genetical effect upon other behavior patterns commonly considered instinctive. There is no reason to assume that so-called instinctive reactions are more dependent upon heredity than noninstinctive responses; hence genetical determination is not a differentiating criterion.

THE MEANING OF GENETICAL DETERMINATION

Behavior which is known to vary with the genotype is often incorrectly defined as "genetically determined" behavior. Although we can show a correlation between certain genes and particular behavior patterns, this is of course no proof of a causal relationship. Many other genes and nongenic factors are always involved in such correlations. This point is nicely illustrated by a series of experiments on audiogenic seizures in mice.

Susceptibility to fatal seizures is high in some inbred strains and low in others [10]. When a high-incidence and low-incidence strain are crossed, the susceptibility of the F_1 generation is intermediate between those of the parental strains. So far the evidence strongly supports the conclusion that seizure incidence is genetically determined. However, the incidence of seizures can be altered without changing the genetic constitution.

This is accomplished by modifying the prenatal environment. Fertilized eggs recovered from the tubes or uterus of a female of one strain and introduced into the uterus of a female of a different strain will sometimes implant normally and produce viable young. This has been done using seizure-susceptible females as donors and seizure-resistant females as hosts. Under such conditions the genetic characteristics of the young are unaltered, but their susceptibility to fatal seizures is lower than that of their own genetic strain and higher than that of the "foster" mothers in whose uteri they developed [8].

Studies of this sort emphasize the important but often neglected fact that postnatal behavior is affected by factors acting upon the organism before birth. As Sontag has pointed out, this is true of human beings as well as lower species.

"Fetal environment may play a part in determining characteristics of the physiological behavior of any newborn infant. We are too often inclined to neglect this source of modification of physiological potential. Too frequently we think of the individual as beginning life only at birth. Yet because it is during the period of intrauterine life that most of the cells of the vital organs are actually formed, it is during this period that 'environmental' factors such as nutrition, oxygen, mother's hormones, etc. are most important in modifying their characteristics" [25, p. 482].

Another fundamental principle illustrated by the results of transplanting fertilized ova is that the uniformity of behavior which characterizes highly inbred strains of animals cannot be ascribed solely to homozygosity, but depends as well upon *minimal variability of the prenatal environment*. More broadly conceived, this principle implies that behavioral similarities and differences observable at birth are in part a product of intrauterine effects.

If forced to relinquish the criterion of genetical control, proponents of the instinct doctrine fall back upon the criterion of the unlearned nature of instinctive acts. Now learning is a process occurring though time, and can only be studied by longitudinal analysis. If instinctive acts are unlearned, their developmental history must differ in some significant fashion from that of a learned response.

THE ONTOGENY OF BEHAVIOR

No bit of behavior can ever be fully understood until its ontogenesis has been described. Had psychologists always recognized this fact, much of the fruitless debate about unlearned behavior could have been avoided.

Perhaps the most widely cited psychological experiment on development and instinctive behavior is that of Carmichael, who studied the swimming behavior of larval amphibians [2]. He reared embryos in a solution which paralyzed the striped muscles but permitted normal growth. Animals that were thus prevented from practicing the swimming response were nevertheless capable of normal swimming when placed in pure water. These findings are often offered as proof of the claim that swimming is instinctive. However, to demonstrate that practice is not essential for the appearance of a response is only the beginning of the analysis. This point is clearly illustrated by certain observations of insect behavior.

Gravid female moths, Hyponomenta padella, lay their eggs on the leaves of the hackberry plant and die shortly thereafter. The eggs hatch, the larvae eat the leaves and eventually become mature. Females of this new generation in turn select hackberry leaves on which to deposit their eggs. Another race of moths prefers apple leaves as an oviposition site. The difference between the two races has been perpetuated, generation after generation, for many centuries. It would appear to be the example par excellence of a genetically controlled behavior trait. But such an explanation is insufficient.

When eggs of the apple-preferring type are transferred to hackberry leaves, the larvae thrive on the new diet. Thirty per cent of the females developing from these larvae show a preference for hackberry leaves when it comes time for them to deposit their eggs [16].

The evidence is of course incomplete. Why only 30 per cent of the insects show a reversal of preference is not clear. It would be illuminating if the same experimental treatment could be repeated on several successive generations. Nevertheless, it appears likely that the adult moth's choice of an oviposition site is influenced by the chemical composition of the food consumed during the larval period [6]. If this interpretation is correct, the data illustrate the fact that a complex behavior pattern may be "unlearned" and still depend upon the individual's previous history.

Comparable examples can be found in the behavior of vertebrates. Stereotyped patterns of behavior appear with great regularity in successive generations under conditions in which practice plays no obvious role. Nonetheless such "species-specific" responses may be dependent upon previous experience of the organism.

The maternal behavior of primiparous female rats reared in isolation is indistinguishable from that of multiparous individuals. Animals with no maternal experience build nests before the first litter is born, clean the young, eat the placenta, and retrieve scattered young to the nest [1]. However, pregnant rats that have been reared in cages containing nothing that can be picked up and transported do not build nests when material is made available. They simply heap their young in a pile in a corner of the cage. Other females that have been reared under conditions preventing them from licking and grooming their own bodies fail to clean their young at the time of parturition [22].

There are undoubtedly many adaptive responses which appear *de novo* at the biologically appropriate time in the absence of preceding practice, but the possibility remains that component parts of a complex pattern have in fact been perfected in different contexts. Whether or not this is the case can only be determined by exhaustive analysis of the ontogeny of the behavior under examination. Nonetheless, to define behavior as "unlearned" in the absence of such analysis is meaningless and misleading.

SUMMARY AND CONCLUSIONS

The concept of instinctive behavior seems to have originated in antiquity in connection with attempts to define a clear-cut difference between man and all other animals. Human behavior was said to be governed by reasoning, and the behavior of animals to depend upon instinct. In his possession of the unique power of reason, man was elevated above all other creatures, and, incidentally, his use of them for his own purposes was thus morally justified.

Christian theologians adopted this point of view and averred that man was given the power of reason so that he could earn his own salvation. Similar privileges could not logically be accorded to lower animals. Therefore they were denied reason and their behavior was explained as a product of divinely implanted instincts. In both sacred and secular philosophies the concept of instinct served a practical purpose, although in no instance was there any attempt to validate it by examination of the empirical evidence.

The concept gained a central position in scientific thinking as a result of the Darwinian movement. Proponents of the evolutionary theory accepted uncritically the assumption that all behavior must be governed by instinct or by reasoning. Their aim was to demonstrate that animals can reason and that men possess instincts. The same dichotomy has persisted in experimental psychology. Attempts to eliminate the instinct concept were unsuccessful because those who made the attempt accepted the idea that all behavior is either acquired or inherited.

No such classification can ever be satisfactory. It rests upon exclusively negative definitions of one side of the dichotomy. It obscures the basic problems involved. It reflects an unnaturally narrow and naive conception of factors shaping behavior.

To remedy the present confused situation it is necessary first to refrain from premature classification of those kinds of behavior that are currently defined as unlearned. Until they have been systematically analyzed, it will remain impossible to decide whether these numerous response patterns belong in one or a dozen different categories.

The analysis that is needed involves two types of approach. One rests upon determination of the relationships existing between genes and behavior. The other consists of studying the development of various behavior patterns in the individual, and determining the number and kinds of factors that normally control the final form of the response.

When these methods have been applied to the various types of behavior which today are called "instinctive," the concept of instinct will disappear, to be replaced by scientifically valid and useful explanations.

REFERENCES

1. BEACH, F. A. The neural basis of innate behavior. I. Effects of cortical lesions upon the maternal be-

havior pattern in the rat. *J. Comp. Psychol.*, 1937, 24, 393-436.

2. CARMICHAEL, L. The development of behavior in vertebrates experimentally removed from the influence of external stimulation. *Psychol. Rev.*, 1927, 34, 34-47.

3. ———. The growth of sensory control of behavior before birth. *Psychol. Rev.*, 1947, 54, 316-324.

4. DENNIS, W. Infant development under conditions of restricted practice. *Genet. psychol. Monogr.*, 1941, 23, 143-189.

5. DUNLAP, K. Are there any instincts? *J. Abnorm. Psychol.*, 1919-20, 14, 35-50.

6. EMERSON, A. E., Ecology, evolution and society. *Amer. Nat.*, 1943, 77, 97-118.

7. FULLER, J. L., and SCOTT, J. P. Heredity and learning ability in infrahuman animals. *Eugenics Quart.*, 1954, 1, 28-43.

8. GINSBURG, B. E., and HOVDA, R. B. On the physiology of gene controlled audiogenic seizures in mice. *Anat. Rec.*, 1947, 99, 65-66.

9. HALL, C. S. The inheritance of emotionality, *Sigma Xi Quart.*, 1938, 26, 17-27.

10. HALL, C. S. Genetic differences in fatal audiogenic seizures between two inbred strains of house mice. *J. Hered.*, 1947, 38, 2-6.

11. HALL, C. S. The genetics of behavior. In S. S. Stevens (Ed.), *Handbook of Experimental Psychology*. New York: Wiley, 1951.

12. HERON, W. T. The inheritance of maze learning ability in rats. *J. Comp. Psychol.*, 1935, 19, 77-89.

13. HERTER, K. Die Beziehungen zwischen Vorzugstemperatur und Hautbeschaffenheit bei Mausen. *Zool. Anz. Suppl.*, 1938, 11, 48-55.

14. HODGSON, R. E. An eight generation experiment in inbreeding swine. *J. Hered.*, 1935, 26, 209-217.

15. HURST, C. C. *Experiments in genetics*. Cambridge: Cambridge Univ. Press., 1925.

16. IMMS, A. D. *Recent Advances in Entymology*. Philadelphia: Blakiston's Sons, 1931.

17. KEELER, C. E., and KING, H. D. Multiple effects of coat color genes in the Norway rat, with special reference to temperament and domestication. *J. Comp. Psychol.*, 1942, 34, 241-250.
18. KUO, Z. Y. A psychology without heredity. *Psychol. Rev.*, 1924, 31, 427-451.
19. LASHLEY, K. S. Experimental analysis of instinctive behavior. *Psychol. Rev.*, 1938, 45, 445-471.
20. MORGAN, C. T. The hoarding instinct. *Psychol. Rev.*, 1947, 54, 335-341.
21. MUNN, N. *Psychological development*. New York: Houghton Mifflin, 1938.
22. RIESS, B. F. The isolation of factors of learning and native behavior in field and laboratory studies. *Ann. N.Y. Acad. Sci.*, 1950, 51, 1093-1102.
23. RUNDQUIST, E. A. The inheritance of spontaneous activity in rats. *J. Comp. Psychol.*, 1933, 16, 415-438.
24. SCOTT, J. P. Genetic differences in the social behavior of inbred strains of mice. *J. Hered.*, 1942, 33, 11-15.
25. SONTAG, L. W. The genetics of differences in psychosomatic patterns in childhood. *Amer. J. Orthopsychiat.*, 1950, 20, 479-489.
26. THOMPSON, W. R. The inheritance of behaviour: behavioural differences in fifteen mouse strains. *Canad. J. Psychol.*, 1953, 7, 145-155.
27. TRYON, R. C. Genetics of learning ability in rats. *Univ. Calif. Publ. Psychol.*, 1929, 4, 71-89.
28. WADDELL, D. Hoarding behavior in the Golden Hamster. *J. Comp. Physiol. Psychol.*, 1951, 44, 383-388.
29. WHITNEY, L. F. Heredity of trail barking propensity of dogs. *J. Hered.*, 1929, 20, 561-562.
30. YERKES, R. M. The heredity of savageness and wildness in rats. *J. Anim. Behav.*, 1913, 3, 286-296.

MAR 28 1968

1541-25